ONLINE MARKETING PRACTICES

ONLINE MARKETING PRACTICES

HARISH CHAURASIA

RAJAT PUBLICATIONS
NEW DELHI - 110 002 (INDIA)

RAJAT PUBLICATIONS
4740/23, Ansari Road, Daryaganj
New Delhi- 110 002 (India)
Phones : 23267924, 9811484973
E-mail: rajat_publication@yahoo.com

Online Marketing Practices

Edition 2026

ISBN 978-81-7880-314-2

PRINTED IN INDIA

Published by Mrs. Seema Wasan for Rajat Publications, New Delhi and Printed at Asian Offset Press, Delhi.

Preface

Marketing includes a variety of activities relating to the distribution and sale of goods and services. Simple marketing practices activities began with the development of an economy where agriculture was not the only form of occupation, and inter-regional trade, including caravan and maritime commerce. Village fairs, town markets, and peddlers were all involved in primitive marketing activities. Later, general stores, travelling sales people, and still later the 20th century chain store became the chief marketing activities. Today, with the advent of computers and the internet in an unprecedented way, online marketing has emerged as the most preferred medium of marketing. Television, radio and newspapers have all played their part in serving to aid managerial practices; it is now the turn of the internet to act as an effective outlet to achieve marketing goals.

The aim of marketing is to acquire, retain and satisfy customers. With the growth of multinational corporations, and the subsequent globalisation, marketing has greatly expanded it scope, many marketing managers take the whole world as their marketplace. Online marketing gives a great impetus to this perception, and very rightly too- for the internet makes information accessible to a wide range of people, transcending geographies, histories, gender, class and age.

However, as this field shows great promise, caution needs to be exercised too. Managers of global, online marketing practices often fail to take into account international differences in the culture, customs and business practices, and quite often fail where they should have succeeded. In addition, recently, some companies that do business online have been caught giving away or selling information about their customers. Several of these companies have guarantees on their websites, claiming customer information will be private. By selling customer information, these companies are breaking their own, publicized policy. Further, many fail managers fail to understand the limitations of the internet. Slow Internet connections can cause difficulties. If companies build overly large or complicated web pages, Internet users may struggle to download the information. Internet marketing does not allow shoppers to touch, smell, taste or try-on tangible goods before making an online purchase. Another limiting factor, particularly with respect to actual buying and selling, is the adequate development (or lack thereof) of electronic payment methods like e-checks, credit cards, etc. All these inadequacies of the internet are to be evaluated before online marketing is taken up in an extensive manner.

This book serves as a one-stop guide for mangers who may feel the need for getting acquainted with all the nuances of online marketing practices, and be informed about the issues concerning these practices. Charting its growth as a popular form of marketing, the book presents a comprehensive discussion of the current trends and developments in this field, taking into account all matters of concern, which have been detailed quite thoroughly. Compendious yet thorough, it is hoped that the book serves well for the readers.

Harish Chaurasia

Contents

1 Introduction

The word marketing has two distinct meanings in modern management practice. It describes:

— *The range of specialist marketing functions* carried out within many organisations. Such functions include market research, brand/product management, public relations and customer service.

— *An approach or concept that can be used as the guiding philosophy* for all functions and activities of an organisation. Such a philosophy encompasses all aspects of a business. Business strategy is guided by an organisation's market and competitor focus and everyone in an organisation should be required to have a customer focus in their job.

The modern marketing concept unites these two meanings and stresses that marketing encompasses the range of organisational functions and processes that seek to determine the needs of target markets and deliver products and services to customers and other key stakeholders such as employees and financial institutions. Increasingly the importance of marketing is being recognised both as a vital function and as a guiding management philosophy within organisations. Marketing has to be seen as the essential focus of all activities within an organisation. The marketing concept should lie at the heart of the organisation, and the actions of directors, managers and employees should be guided by its philosophy.

Modern marketing requires organisations to be committed to a market/customer orientation. All parts of the organisation should co-ordinate activities to ensure that customer needs are met efficiently, effectively and profitably. Marketing encompasses activities traditionally seen as the sole domain of accountants, production, human resources management (HRM) and information technology (IT). Many of these functions had little regard for customer considerations. Increasingly such functions are being reorientated, evidenced by the importance of initiatives such as Total Quality Management (TQM), Business Process Reengineering, Just in Time (JIT) and supply chain management. Individuals' functional roles are undergoing change, from being solely functional to having a greater emphasis on process. Individuals are therefore being encouraged to become part-time marketers. Processes have a significant impact on an organisation' s ability to service its customers' needs.

The Internet can be applied by companies as an integral part of the modern marketing concept since:

— It can be used to support the full range of organisational functions and processes that deliver products and services to customers and other key stakeholders.

— It is a powerful communications medium that can act as a 'corporate glue' that integrates the different functional parts of the organisation.

— It facilitates information management, which is now increasingly recognised as a critical marketing support tool to strategy formulation and implementation.

— The future role of the Internet should form part of the vision of a company since its future impact will be significant to most businesses.

Without adequate information, organisations are at a disadvantage with respect to competitors and the external environment. Up-to-date, timely and accessible information about the industry, markets, new technology, competitors and customers is a critical factor in an organisation' s ability to plan and compete in an increasingly competitive marketplace.

Theodore Levitt, writing in the *Harvard Business Review*, outlined the factors that underlie the demise of many organisations and at best seriously weaken their longer-term competitiveness. These factors still provide a timely reminder of traps that should be avoided when embarking on Internet marketing.

— Wrongly defining which business they are in.

— Focusing on:

— products ;

  — production;

  — technology ;

  — selling ; rather than:

  — customer needs ; and

  — market opportunities.

— Unwillingness to innovate and 'creatively destruct' existing product/service lines.

— Short-sightedness in terms of strategic thinking.

— The lack of a strong and visionary CEO.

— Giving marketing only 'stepchild status', behind finance, production and technology.

Any organisation that sees and hence defines its business in anything other than customerbenefit terms has not taken the first step in achieving a market orientation. Any organisation that defines its business by what it produces is said to be suffering from 'marketing myopia'. Such myopia results from a company having a short-sighted and narrow view of the business that it is in.

If Internet marketing is to become integrated and fully established as a strategic marketing management tool, then the focus of attention needs to move towards understanding its broader applications within the total marketing process rather than just using it as a communication and selling tool. This is not to detract from the capability of the Internet to communicate and sell, but recognises that this is only one important aspect of the marketing process to which the Internet can contribute. The danger for those currently considering developing Internet technology is that the focus of such involvement will be too narrow and the true power of the Internet and its potential contribution to the marketing process will be missed.

What then, is Internet marketing? Internet marketing or Internet-based marketing can be defined as the use of the Internet and related digital technologies to achieve marketing objectives and support the modern marketing concept. These technologies include the Internet media and other digital media such as wireless mobile media, cable and satellite.

In practice, Internet marketing will include the use of a company web site in conjunction with online promotional techniques such as search engines, banner advertising, direct e-mail and links or services from other web sites to acquire new customers and provide services to existing customers that help develop the customer relationship. However, for Internet marketing to be successful there is a necessity of integration with traditional media such as Print and TV, and this will be a consistent theme in this book.

E-MARKETING

The term 'Internet marketing' tends to refer to an external perspective of how the Internet can be used in conjunction with traditional media to acquire and deliver services to customers. An alternative term is e-marketing or electronic marketing that can be considered to have a broader scope since this refers to the Internet, interactive digital TV and mobile marketing together with other technology approaches such as database marketing and electronic customer relationship management (CRM) to achieve marketing objectives. It has both an internal and external perspective considering how internal and external marketing processes and communications can be improved through information and communications technology.

As with many terms with the 'e' prefix, return to an original definition of the topic to more fully understand what e-marketing involves. The definition of marketing by the Chartered Institute of Marketing is:

> *Marketing is the management process responsible for identifying, anticipating and satisfying customer requirements profitability*

This definition emphasises the focus of marketing on the customer, while at the same time implying a need to link to other business operations to achieve this profitability. Smith and Chaffey note that Internet technology can be used to support these aims as follows:

— *Identifying* -the Internet be used for marketing research to find out customers needs and wants ;

— *Anticipating* - the Internet provides an additional channel by which customers can access information and make purchases—understanding this demand is key to governing resource allocation to e-marketing.

— Satisfying - a key success factor in e-marketing is achieving customer satisfaction through the electronic channel, this raises issues such as is the site easy to use, does it perform adequately, what is the standard of associated customer service and how are physical products dispatched? These issues of customer relationship management.

A broader definition of marketing has been developed by Dibb, Simkin, Pride and Ferrell:

> Marketing consists of individual and organisational activities that facilitate and expedite satisfying exchange relationships in a dynamic environment through the creation, distribution, promotion and pricing of goods, services and ideas.

Many organisations began the process of Internet marketing with the development of web sites in the form of brochureware or electronic brochures introducing their organisations' products and services, but are now enhancing them to add value to the full range of marketing functions. Stage models of development of Internet marketing services, which start with brochureware sites, that can be used to assess and inform an organisations current and future application of Internet Marketing. Another key aspect of Interent marketing planning is using the Internet for what it is best suited—reaching particular types of customers using innovative selling techniques.

E-COMMERCE AND E-BUSINESS

The terms e-commerce and e-business are often used in a similar context to Internet marketing, but what are the differences between these terms and do the finer distinctions between them matter to the practitioner? In fact, the differences are significant and do matter, since managers within an organisation require a consistent understanding of the opportunities to enable their organisation to have a cohesive strategy to best utilise new technology.

Electronic commerce (E-commerce) is often thought to simply refer to buying and selling using the Internet; people immediately think of consumer retail purchases from companies such as Amazon. However, e-commerce involves much more than electronically mediated *financial* transactions between organisations and customers. Many commentators now refer to e-commerce as both *financial and informational* electronically mediated transactions between an organisation and any third-party it deals with. By this definition, nonfinancial transactions such as customer enquiries and support are also considered to be part of e-commerce. Kalakota and Whinston refer to a range of different perspectives for ecommerce:

— *A communications perspective* - the delivery of information, products/services or payment by electronic means.

— *A business process perspective* - the application of technology towards the automation of business transactions and workflows.

— *A service perspective* - enabling cost cutting at the same time as increasing the speed and quality of service delivery.

— *An online perspective* - the buying and selling of products and information online.

Zwass uses a broad definition of e-commerce noting the significance of information transfer. He refers to it as:

> 'the sharing of business information, maintaining business relationships, and conducting business transactions by means of telecommunications networks'.

The UK government also uses a broad definition:

> 'E-commerce is the exchange of information across electronic networks, at any stage in the supply chain, whether within an organisation, between businesses, between businesses and consumers, or between the public and private sector, whether paid or unpaid'.

All these definitions imply that electronic commerce is not solely restricted to the actual buying and selling of products, but also pre-sale and post-sales activities across the supply chain.

When evaluating the impact of e-commerce on an organisation' s marketing, it is instructive to identify the role of buy-side and sell-side e-commerce transactions. Sell-side e-commerce refers to transactions involved with selling products to an organisation' s customers. Internet marketing is used directly to support sell-side e-commerce. Buy-side ecommerce refers to business-to-business transactions to procure resources needed by an organisation from its suppliers. This is typically the responsibility of those in the operational and procurement functions of an organisation. Remember though, that each e-commerce transaction can be considered from two perspectives: sell-side from the perspective of the selling organisation and buy-side from the perspective of the buying organisation. So for organisational marketing understand the drivers and barriers to buy-side ecommerce in order to accommodate the needs of organisational buyers.

Different types of e-commerce, what then, is e-business? Let start from the definition by IBM, who was one of the first suppliers to coin the term:

> e-business (e' biz' nis)
>
> The transformation of key business processes through the use of Internet technologies.

The key business processes referred to in the IBM definition are the organisational processes. They include research and development, marketing, manufacturing and inbound and outbound logistics. Complete activity 1.1 to gain an appreciation of the type of processes involved. The buy-side e-commerce processes with suppliers and the sell-side e-commerce processes involving exchanges with distributors and customers can also be considered to be key businesses processes.

Marketing Processes in the E-business (WEB)

To highlight how Internet technologies can be used to support marketing.

Business or consumer model

It is now commonplace to describe Internet marketing opportunities in terms of whether an organisation is transacting with consumers. Two additional types of transaction, those where consumers transact directly with other consumers (C2C) and where initiate trading with companies (C2B). Note that the C2C and C2B monikers are less widely used, but they do highlight significant differences between Internet-based commerce and earlier forms of commerce. Consumer-to-consumer interactions were relatively rare, but are now very common in the form of customer support and feedback -the community components of sites and online auctions. Indeed, Hoffman and Novak suggest that C2C interactions are a key characteristic of the Internet that is important for companies to take into account C2C interactions.

Important C2C interactions

To highlight the relevance of C2C transactions to B2C companies. Consult with fellow students and share experience of C2C interactions online. Think of C2C both on independent sites and organisational sites. How can C2C communications assist these organisations?

BENEFITS OF INTERNET MARKETING

The key reason why many companies are seeking to harness the Internet. The reason is an additional source of revenue made possible by an alternative marketing and distribution channel. The marketing opportunities of using the Internet can be appreciated by applying the strategic marketing grid for exploring opportunities for new markets and products. The Internet can potentially be used to achieve each of the four strategic directions as follows:

— *Market penetration.* The Internet can be used to sell more existing products into existing markets. This can be achieved by using the power of the Internet for advertising products to increase awareness of products and the profile of a company amongst potential customers in an existing market. This is a relatively conservative use of the Internet.

— *Market development.* Here the Internet is used to sell into new markets, taking advantage of the low cost of advertising internationally without the necessity for a supporting sales infrastructure in the customers' country. This is a relatively conservative use of the Internet, but it does require the overcoming of the barriers to becoming an exporter or operating in a greater number of countries.

— *Product development.* New products or services are developed which can be delivered by the Internet.

These are typically information products such as market reports which can be purchased using electronic commerce. This is innovative use of the Internet.

— *Diversification*. In this sector, new products are developed which are sold into new markets.

DTI has identified different types of drivers or benefits why companies adopt ecommerce. The main drivers for sell-side e-commerce are:

— *Cost/efficiency drivers*

  — Increasing speed with which goods can be despatched

  — Reduced sales costs

  — Reduced operating costs

— *Competitiveness drivers*

  — Customer demand

  — Improving the range and quality of services offered

  — Avoid losing market share to businesses already using e-commerce

The lure of new sales and the threat of market share erosion has driven many companies on to the Internet, but there are many other benefits of establishing an Internet presence. Consider the example of the parcel courier companies. These companies now provide a range of customer services over the Internet which were traditionally delivered by telephone operators, thus reducing operating costs. In such situations, the online services may give better 24 hour, 7 days a week, 365 days of the year customer service if measured by convenience, but some customers will want the option of the personal touch, and phone services must be provided for this type of customer. Many companies will also reduce the costs of the printing and distribution of promotional material, price lists and other marketing communications.

In addition to increased sales and reduced costs, the Internet can be used to advantage in all of the marketing functions, for example:

— *Sales.* Achieved through increasing awareness of brands and products, supporting buying decisions and enabling online purchase.

— *Marketing communications.* The use of the web site for the range of marketing communication.

— *Customer service.* Supplementing phone operators with information available online and other techniques.

— *Public relations.* The Internet can be used as a new channel for public relations (PR) and provides the opportunity to publish the latest news on products, markets and people.

— *Marketing research.* Through search engines and e-mail alert services, the Internet enables more efficient techniques for finding a range of market information. It also enables new methods for collecting primary research online through focus groups and online questionnaires.

The Internet also changes the way in which companies do business with their trading partners.The benefits of an Internet presence can be summarised using the '6Cs' of, for example, Bocij et al.:

— *Cost reduction.* Achieved through reducing the need for sales and marketing enquiries to be handled by telephone operators and the reduced need for printing and distributing marketing communications material, which is instead published on the web site.

- — *Capability.* The Internet provides new opportunities for new products and services and for exploiting new markets.
- — *Competitive advantage.* If a company introduces new capabilities before its competitors, then it will achieve an advantage until its competitors have the same capability. For example, customers who transferred to Federal Express because of its new Internet services are likely to be less disposed to revert to an existing courier since they are 'locked in' to using the particular tools provided by Federal Express.
- — *Communications improvement.* These include improved communications with customers, staff, suppliers and distributors.
- — *Control.* The Internet and intranets may provide better marketing research through tracking of customer behaviour and the way in which staff deliver services.
- — *Customer service improvement.* Provided by interactive queries of databases containing.

RISE OF INTERNET TECHNOLOGY

Marketers require a basic understanding of Internet technology in order to discuss the implementation of e-marketing with partners. Knowing some of the pitfalls is useful also. The Internet has existed since the late 1960s when a limited number of computers were connected in the United States to form the ARPAnet. This was mainly used to enable academics and military personnel to exchange defence information.

Why then has the Internet only recently been widely adopted for business purposes? The recent dramatic growth in the use of the Internet has occurred because of the development of the World Wide Web. This became a commercial proposition in 1993 after development of the original concept by Tim Berners-Lee, a British scientist working at CERN in Switzerland in 1989. The World Wide Web changed the Internet from a difficult-to-use tool for academics and technicians to an easy-to-use tool for finding information for businesses and consumers. The World Wide Web is an interlinked publishing medium for displaying graphic and text information. This information is stored on web server computers and then accessed by users who run web browser programmes, which display the information and allow users to select links to access other web sites.

The technical name for web addresses is uniform or universal resource locators (URLs). URLs can be thought of as a standard method of addressing similar to postal or ZIP codes that make it straightforward to find the name of a site. The domain name refers to the name of the web server and is usually selected to be the same as the name of the company and the extension will indicate its type. The extension is also commonly known as the global top level domain (gTLD). Note that gTLDs are currently under discussion and there are proposals for adding new types such as.store and.firm.

The 'filename.html' part of the web address refers to an individual web page, for example 'products.html' for a web page summarising companies' products. When a web address is typed in without a filename, for example www.bt.com, the browser automatically assumes the user is looking for the home page, that by convention is referred to as index.html. When creating sites, it is therefore vital to name the home page index.html.

The Internet enables communication between millions of connected computers world-wide. Information is transmitted from client PCs whose users request services to server computers that hold information and host business applications that deliver the services in response to requests. As such, the Internet is a large-scale client/server system. By end 2000, Nua compilations estimated that worldwide, there were over 450 million users of clients accessing over 30 million web sites hosted on servers.

The client PCs within homes and businesses are connected to the Internet via local Internet Service Providers (ISPs) who, in turn, are linked to larger ISPs with connection to the major national and international infrastructure or backbones. In the UK, at the London Internet Exchange which is the Docklands area of East London, a facility exists to connects multiple backbones of the major ISPs within the UK onto a single high-speed link out of the UK into Europe and through to the US. These high speed links can be thought of as the motorways on the 'information superhighway' while the links provided from ISPs to consumers are equivalent to slow country roads.

Importance of Web Page Standards

The information, graphics and interactive elements that make up the web pages of a site are collectively referred to as content. Different standards exist for text, graphics and multimedia. The saying 'content is king' is often applied to the World Wide Web, since the content will determine the experience of the customer and whether they will return to a web site in future.

Text Information and Hypertext Markup Language (HTML)

Web page text has many of the formatting options

available in a word processor. These include applying fonts, emphasis and placing information in tables. Formatting is possible since the web browser applies these formats according to instructions that are contained in the file that makes up the web page. This is usually written in HTML or hypertext markup language. HTML is an international standard established by the World Wide Web Consortium intended to ensure that any web page authored according to the definitions in the standard will appear the same in any web browser.

A simple example of HTML is given for a simplified home page for a B2B company. The HTML code used to construct pages has codes or instruction tags such as <TITLE> to indicate to the browser what is displayed. The <TITLE> tag indicates what appears at the top of the web browser window. Each starting tag has a corresponding end tag usually marked by a '/', for example <B>plastics</B> to embolden plastics.

The simplicity of HTML compared to traditional programming languages makes it possible for simple web pages to be developed by non-specialists such as marketing assistants, particularly if templates complex parts of the page are provided. Interactive forms and brochures and online sales are more complex and usually require some programming expertise, although tools are available to simplify these.

Text Information and Data -Extensible Markup Language (XML)

When the early version of HTML was designed by Tim Berners-Lee at CERN, he based it on the existing standard for representation of documents. This standard was SGML, the Standard Generalised Markup Language that was ratified by the ISO in 1986. SGML uses tags to identify the different elements of a documents such as title and chapters. HTML used a similar approach, for example the tag for title is <TITLE>. While HTML proved powerful in providing a standard method of displaying information, that was easy to learn, it was purely presentational. It lacked the ability to describe the data on web pages.

A metadata language providing data about data contained within pages would be much more powerful. These weaknesses have been acknowledged, and in an effort co-ordinated by the World Wide Web consortium, the first XML or eXtensible Markup Language was produced in February 1998. This is also based on SGML. The key word describing XML is 'extensible'. This means that new markup tags can be created that facilitate the searching and exchange of information. The tags can effectively act as a standard set of database field descriptions so that data can be exchanged through B2B exchanges.

<metadata>

Literally, data about data - a format describing the structure and content of data

The importance of XML are indicated by its incorporation by Microsoft into its BizTalk server for B2B integration and the creation of ebXML standard by rivals Sun Microsystems. It is also the main standard for data exchange for CommerceOne B2B Marketplace and industry standards, for example transferring data between companies in the chemical process industry. In future, XML may become increasingly important for search engines.

<startbox>

Mini case - example XML for Online Marketplace catalogue

This example is taken from the Commerce One xCBL 3.0

statndard for Publishing catalogue data. It can be seen that specific tags are used to idenity:

— Product ID.

— Manufacturer.

— Long and short description.

— Attributes of product and associated picture.

There is no pricing information in this example.

```
<CatalogData>
<Product>
<Action Value="Delete"/>
<ProductID>118003-008</ProductID>
</Product>
<Product Type="Good" SchemaCategoryRef="C43171801">
<ProductID>140141-002</ProductID>
<UOM><UOMCoded>EA</UOMCoded></UOM>
<Manufacturer>Compaq</Manufacturer>
<LeadTime>2</LeadTime>
<CountryOfOrigin>
<Country><CountryCoded>US</CountryCoded></Country>
</CountryOfOrigin>
<ShortDescription xml:lang="en">Armada M700 PIII 500
12GB</ShortDescription>
<LongDescription xml:lang="en">
```

This light, thin powerhouse delivers no-compromise performance in a sub-five pound form factor. Size and Weight(HxWxD): 12.4 X 9.8 X 1.1 in 4.3—4.9 lbs Processor:

500-MHZ Intel Pentium III Processor with 256K integrated cache Memory: 128MB of RAM, expandable to 576MB Hard Drive: 12.0GB Removable SMART Hard Drive Display Graphics: 14.1-inch colour TFT with 1024 x 768resolution

Communication: Mini-PCI V.90 Modem/Nic ComboOperating

System: Dual Installation of Microsoft Windows 95 & Microsoft Windows 98

</LongDescription>

<ProductAttachment>

<AttachmentURL>file:\5931.jpg</AttachmentURL>

<AttachmentPurpose>PicName</AttachmentPurpose>

<AttachmentMIMEType>jpg</AttachmentMIMEType>

</ProductAttachment>

<ObjectAttribute>

<AttributeID> Processor Speed</AttributeID>

<AttributeValue>500MHZ</AttributeValue>

</ObjectAttribute>

<ObjectAttribute>

<AttributeID>Battery Life</AttributeID>

<AttributeValue>6 hours</AttributeValue>

</ObjectAttribute>

</Product>

Graphical Images

Graphics produced by graphic designers or captured using digital cameras can be readily incorporated into web pages as images. GIF (Graphics Interchange Format) and JPEG (Joint Photographics Experts Group) refer to two standard file formats most commonly used to present images on web pages. GIF files are limited to 256 colours and are best used for small simple graphics such as banner adverts while JPEG are best used for larger images where image quality is important such as photographs. Both formats use image compression technology to minimise the size of downloaded files.

Animated Graphical Information

GIF files can also be used for interactive banner adverts. Plug-ins are additional programmes sometimes referred to as helper applications that work in association with the web browser to provide features not present in the basic web browser. The best known plug-ins are probably that for Adobe Acrobat that is used to display documents in.pdf format and the Macromedia Flash and Shockwave products for producing interactive graphics.

Audio and Video Standards

Traditionally sound and video or rich media have been stored as the Microsoft standards.WAV and.AVI. A newer sound format for music is MP3. These formats are used on some web sites, but they are not appropriate for site such as the BBC, since the user would have to wait until the whole clip to download before hearing or viewing it. Streaming media are now used for many multimedia sites since they enable video or audio to start playing within a few seconds—it is not necessary for the whole file to be downloaded before it can be played. Formats for streaming media have been established by Real Networks.

Internet Access Software Applications

Over its lifetime, many tools have been developed to help

find, send and receive information across the Internet. Web browsers used to access the World Wide Web are the latest of these applications. The relevance of some of the more commonly used tools to the modern organisation. The other tools have either been superseded by the use of the World Wide Web or are of less relevance from a business perspective. The application of the Internet for marketing the use of e-mail and the World Wide Web since these tools are now most commonly used by businesses for digital marketing. Many of the other tools such as e-mail, IRC and newsgroups, that formerly needed special software to access them, are now available from the WWW.

Internet to Intranets and Extranets

Intranet and extranet are two terms that have arisen in the 1990s to describe applications of Internet technologies that do not only involve communicating with customers, but rather with company staff and third parties such as suppliers and distributors. While everyone connected to the Internet can access a company Internet web site, only those who have been given authorisation can access an intranet or extranet. It can be seen that an intranet is effectively a private-company Internet with access available to staff only. An extranet permits access to trusted third parties, and the Internet provides global access. Extranets provide exciting opportunities to communicate with major customers since tailored information such as special promotions, electronic catalogues and order histories can be provided on a web page personalised for each customer.

Opportunities for using intranets and extranets to support the marketing process can be divided in two different ways.

— the Internet can be used for marketing communications both within and beyond the company. As well as using the Internet to communicate with customers, companies find that internal use of an intranet or use of an extranet facilitate communication and control between staff, suppliers and distributors.

— the Internet, intranet and extranet can be applied at different levels of management within a company. Potential marketing applications of both the Internet and intranet for supporting marketing at different levels of managerial decision making.

Differences Between Internet Marketing Communications and Traditional Marketing Communications

Internet marketing differs from conventional marketing communications because of the digital medium used for communications. The Internet and other digital media such as digital television, satellite and mobile phones create new forms and models for information exchange. A useful summary of the differences between these new media and traditional media has been developed by McDonald and Wilson which they describe as the '6Is of the e-marketing mix'. Note that these can be used as a strategic analysis tool, but they are not used in this context here.

The 6Is are useful since they highlight factors that apply to practical aspects of Internet marketing such as personalisation, direct response and marketing research, but also strategic issues of industry restructuring and integrated channel communications. By considering each of these facets of the new media, marketing managers can develop marketing plans that accommodate the characteristics of the new media. This presentation of the '6Is', is an interpretation of these factors using new examples and diagrams to illustrate these concepts.

Effect of Interactivity

Deighton was one of the first authors to summarise the key characteristics of the Internet. He identifies the following characteristics inherent in a digital medium:

— the customer initiates contact;

— the customer is seeking information ;

— it is a high intensity medium—the marketer will have 100 per cent of the individual' s attention when he or she is viewing a web site;

— a company can gather and store the response of the individual;

— individual needs of the customer can be addressed and taken into account in future dialogues.

Traditional media are predominantly *push media* where the marketing message is broadcast from company to customer and other stakeholders. During this process, there is limited interaction with the customer, although interaction is encouraged in some cases such as the direct response advert or mail-order campaign. On the Internet, it is usually a customer who initiates contact and is seeking information on a web site.

Effect of Intelligence

The Internet can be used as a relatively low cost method of collecting marketing research, particularly about customer perceptions of products and services. In the competitions referred to above Nescafe are able to profile their customers on the basis of the information received in questionnaires. The Internet can be used to create two-way feedback which does not usually occur in other media. Financial services provider Egg collects information about their online service levels through a questionnaire that is continuously available in the customer service part of their site. What is significant is that the company responds via the web site to the main concerns from customer; if the length of time it takes to reply to customer service e-mails is seen as a problem it will explain what the organisation is trying to do to resolve this problem.

A wealth of marketing research information is also available from the web site itself, since every time a user clicks on a link this is recorded in a transaction log file summarising what information on the site the customer is interested in. Since these log files quickly grow to be many thousands of lines long, analysis software tools are needed to summarise the information contained within them. Log file analysers, of which Webtrends is the most widely used, will highlight which type of products or promotions customers are responding to and how patterns vary through time. This enables companies to respond in realtime to buyer behaviour. UK e-tailer Jungle.com uses this technique to change the offers on its home page if customers are not responding to a special offer.

Effect of Individualisation

Another important feature of the interactive marketing communications referred to above is that they can be tailored to the individual unlike traditional media where the same message tends to be broadcast to everyone. The process of tailoring is also referred to as *personalisation* and is an important aspect of achieving customer relationship management online. Personalisation is often achieved through extranets which are set up with key accounts to manage the buying and after-sales processes. Dell has set up 'Premier Pages' for key accounts such as the Abbey National where special offers and bespoke customer support are delivered. Another example of personalisation is that achieved by business-to-business e-tailer RS Components.

Every customer who accesses their system is profiled according to their area of product interest and information describing their role in the buying unit. When they next visit the site information will be displayed relevant to their product interest, for example office products and promotions if this is what was selected. This is an example of what is known as mass customisation where generic customer information is supplied for particular segments i.e. the information is not unique to individuals, but to those with a common interest. The online booksellers such as Amazon use this approach to communicate new books to groups of customers. Gardeners for instance, who have previously purchased a gardening book, will receive a standard e-mail advertising the latest gardening tome. This is again mass customisation.

Effect of Integration

The Internet provides further scope for integrated marketing communications. When assessing the success of a web site, the role of the Internet in communicating with customers and other partners can best be considered from two perspectives. First organisation to customer direction, how does the Internet complement other channels in communication of proposition for the company' s products and services to new and existing customers with a view to generating new leads and retaining existing customers? Second customer to organisation, how can the Internet complement other channels to deliver customer service to these customers? Many companies are now considering how they integrate e-mail response and web-site call-back into their existing call-centre or customer service operation. This may require a substantial investment in training and new software.

Some practical examples of how the Internet can be used as an integrated communications tool are as follows:

— The Internet can be used as a direct response tool enabling customers to respond to offers and promotions publicised in other media.

— The web site can have a direct response or call-back facility built into it. The Automobile Association have a feature where a customer service representative will contact a customer by phone when the customer fills in their name, phone number and a suitable time to ring.

— The Internet can be used to support the buying decision even if the purchase does not occur via the web site. For example, Dell has a prominent web-specific phone number on their web site that encourages customers to ring a representative in the call-centre to place their order. This has the benefits that Dell are less likely to lose the business of customers who are anxious about the security of online ordering and Dell can track sales that result partly from the web site according to the number of callers on this line. Considering how a customer changes from one channel to another during the buying process is referred to as mixed-mode buying. It is a key aspect of devising online marketing communications since the customer should be supported in changing from one channel to another.

— Customer information delivered on the web site must be integrated with other databases of customer and order information such as those accessed via staff in the call-centre to provide what Seybold calls a '360 degree view of the customer'.

The Internet can be used to support customer service.

Integrating online and off-line communications

To highlight differences in marketing communications introduced through the use of the Internet as a channel and the need to integrate these communications with existing channels.

List communications between PC vendor and a home customer over the lifetime of a product such as a PC. Include both communications using the Internet and traditional media. Refer to channel swapping alternatives in the buying decision.

Concept of Industry Restructuring

Disinteremediation and reintemediation, are key concepts of industry restructuring that should be considered by any company developing an e-marketing strategy and are explored. For the marketer defining their companies communications strategy it becomes very important to consider a companies representation on these intermediary sites by answering questions such as 'which intermediaries should be represented on?' and 'how do offerings compare to those of competitors in terms of features, benefits and price?'

Independence of Location

Electronic media also introduce the possibility to increase the reach of company communications to the global market. This gives opportunities to sell into international markets that may not have been previously possible. Scott Bader, a business-to-business supplier of polymers and chemicals for the paints and coatings industry, can now target countries beyond the 40 or so it has traditionally sold to via a network of local agents and franchises. The Internet makes it possible to sell to a country without a local sales or customer service force. In such situations and with the restructuring in conjunction with disintermediation and reintermediation, strategists also need to carefully consider channel conflicts that may arise. If a customer is buying direct from a company in another country rather than via the agent, this will marginalise the business of the local agent who may want some recompense for sales efforts or may look to partner with competitors.

Conversion Internet Marketing

One of the key features of Internet marketing using the web is that the customer has to consciously decide to visit a particular site according to the particular information or experience he or she is seeking. The problem of encouraging site visitors is compounded since it is difficult for potential customers to find a company web site. It is estimated that there are over one billion web pages amongst which a company is competing for the attention of customers. It follows that promoting the location of the web site is critical for companies.

The implication for marketers is that Internet marketing communications strategies for most companies should focus on the acquisition of site visitors, converting them to a required action on the site and then retaining these visitors. Internet marketers seek to use conversion marketing to convert as many *potential* site visitors into *actual* visitors and then convert these into customers and repeat visitors. A widely quoted conceptual measurement framework based on the industrial marketing concepts of purchasing decision processes and hierarchy of effects models has been proposed by Berthon et al. which can be applied for conversion marketing. The model assesses efficiency of off-line and online communications in drawing the prospect through different stages of the buying decision. The main measures defined in the model were:

— *Awareness efficiency.* Target web-users/all web-users.

— *Locatability/attractability efficiency.* Number of individual visits/number of seekers.

— *Contact efficiency.* Number of active visitors/Number of visits.

— *Conversion efficiency.* Number of purchases/number of active visits.

— *Retention efficiency.* Number of repurchases/number of purchases.

This model is instructive for improving Internet marketing within an organisation since these different types of conversion efficiency are key to understanding how effective online and off-line marketing communications are in achieving marketing outcomes. The original model of Berthon et al. from Chaffey, which highlights the key conversion metrics of attraction efficiency and conversion efficiency. It shows key traffic or audience measures and key conversion efficiency ratios. The model has been revised to reflect current nomenclature. Also the original work was focused on conversion to purchase—the model is more widely applicable since it applies to any marketing outcome achieved on site, whether this is a new lead from a potential customer, a competition entrant or a sale.

2

Internet Marketing

Internet marketing is the component of marketing that deals with the planning, pricing, promotion, and distribution of your products and services online. Good Internet marketing strategies clearly communicate a firm's unique selling proposition, or the unique collection of benefits that creates value for its customers. Everything you do to promote your business online is Internet marketing.

Benefits of Internet Marketing

Here are some examples of the time and cost-saving benefits of using the Internet to market your products or services:

— The Internet is the widest channel of communication available to small businesses. It can help level the playing field for small businesses on a limited budget that seek to compete in large markets. No other communications medium enables you to operate a business from your home, while giving a small business the appearance of a larger, more established operation.

— Marketing your product or service online offers the opportunity for increased communication with your target market through techniques such as interactive websites, email newsletters, online surveys and forms, blogs, and discussion groups. The Internet allows you to collect immediate feedback from your client base with little out-of-pocket expense.

— Print marketing materials and advertising strategies can be expensive to produce and traditionally have a short shelf life. Internet marketing techniques such as websites, banner ads and email newsletters, can be produced at a reasonable cost, can contain more timely information than print brochures, and can be immediately and cost-effectively updated as your business changes.

Finding success online is no different from finding it off-line. Choosing the right product or service and designing an appropriate online and off-line marketing mix are key to successful Internet marketing.

Steps to Successful Marketing

Successful marketing on the Internet is not just about advertising your website in Google or buying banner ads on other websites. Without a quality product or service and a well developed website, a banner ad.

To succeed online, you must develop a comprehensive plan that includes the following:

— A solid business model and great products or services

— An effectively designed website with sales as an objective

— An online marketing strategy that suits your audience and fits your budget

Appearance of Internet Marketing

No matter what your business, Internet marketing should form part of your marketing mix—how large a part will depend on your particular needs and budget. The tools you use to develop your online presence and drive traffic to your website will also depend on your particular business and target market demographics. Internet marketing is a fast-changing industry that readily adapts to improvements in technology. Therefore, there are always new marketing tools available to small businesses.

Website Development & SEO

Designing and building a website is only one aspect of bringing your business online. With billions of websites on the Internet, it's just as important that you ensure people can find your website. And, since most website traffic still comes from search engines and directories—98% of Internet users claim they use search engines regularly—you may want to focus your initial web marketing efforts on search engine optimization. Search engines such as Google and Yahoo index billions of web pages and rank them according to complex algorithms that assess a page's accessibility, its relevance based on specific search terms or keywords, and importance indicated by the number of sites that link to it. Search engine optimization (SEO) refers to the work that is done to a website to ensure it gets noticed and ranked highly by search engines. Ideally, you want to strive for a top ten ranking, because studies have shown that most search engine users don't scroll past the first page of results.

Keep in mind, SEO is not an exact science, and as such, SEO specialists often use slightly different methods. That said, generally, SEO includes:

— Building a website using "search engine friendly" coding techniques that minimise the use of Flash and frames

— Researching appropriate search terms—called "keywords" or "keyword phrases"—that fit the target market

— Incorporating keyword-rich content into a website's domain name, meta tags, title tags, alt tags, headings and overall content, and ensuring that content is updated regularly.

— Submitting the website address to search engines

— Developing a reciprocal linking strategy with other websites to grow quality inbound links to the site

Site to Search Engines and Directories

Some engines will find and list your site on their own, some require you to register, and others offer a combination of both. Further, some registration procedures are free and some require that you pay to be listed.

In short, there are two kinds of search engines out there.

— *Crawler-based search engines*, like Google, are those that use automated, computer generated indexing systems. These engines use software to "crawl" your website, index relevant content and keywords, and follow links. The software will look for patterns or repetition in your content in order to determine the website's purpose. These engines do not require you to do anything other than upload your "optimised" website to the Internet and wait for them to find it. Since it may take a few months for the engines to crawl your site naturally, however, they also offer you the opportunity to submit your URL in the hope of being ranked more quickly. Failing that, you can always purchase paid placement in some engines such as Google and Overture.

— *Human-powered directories,* like Yahoo's Directory, are those that use humans to index website listings. These engines are actually called directories and require you to submit your URL and wait for the directory editors to assess and index your site based on perceived relevancy. Sometimes this procedure is free, and sometimes you have to pay a fee for the privilege of being reviewed.

Here is a list of the most popular search engines and directories you'll want to consider:

— Google - www.google.ca/com.

— Yahoo - www.yahoo.ca/com.

— MSN - www.msn.com.

— Teoma - www.teoma.com.

— Overture - www.overture.com.

— Open Directory - http://dmoz.org/.

— AltaVista - www.altavista.com.

— Inktomi - www.inktomi.com.

Importance of Growing Inbound Links

It should be emphasized that the more quality inbound links your website has, the more likely it is to be deemed "important" by the search engines. Therefore, a good SEO package includes the development of a quality linking strategy. This is a technique that connects your website to other relevant websites, through the placement of text-based links. To begin, consider linking with complementary businesses and industry associations. This is as easy as sending out a personalised email requesting a link on another website. Keep in mind, particularly for those just starting out, linking strategies are usually reciprocal. So, be prepared to offer a link on your own site in exchange for the link you hope to receive.

Online Advertising Models

In addition to optimising your website and increasing your site traffic through search engines, consider advertising on third-party websites and in search engines using a combination of banner advertisements and text links.

— Graphical banner advertisements, pop-ups and text based ads are online ads that are placed on third-party websites that link back to your website. The ads are designed to encourage users to click through to your site to learn more and, ultimately, to buy. These ads can be set up for a fee—pay-per-click, payper-lead, pay-per-sale—or they can be part of a reciprocal ad exchange with an online "partner," where you place your partner's ad on your website in exchange for your partner doing the same.

— Paid advertising in search engines. Some search engines offer marketers the opportunity to buy guaranteed search engine listings through the purchase of keywords. Google, for example, has a paid solution called Adwords—think of it as pay-per-click advertising in its simplest form. Google allows advertisers to bid for "sponsored links"—paid listings across the top and down the right side of Google's search results—on a per-bid basis. As an advertiser, you decide what keywords you want to "bid" on, how much you are willing to pay per click back to your website, and how much you are willing to pay in total per day—USD $1? $10? More? Less? It's completely up to you.

Paid search engine listings are a quick, cost-effective way to get your site into search engines, without the wait associated with "natural" ranking.

Third-Party Websites

Another, often overlooked, but cost-saving method of marketing your business online is by publishing editorials in third-party e-zines, e-newsletters and on information-based websites. Just as editorials in off-line media can help position you as an expert in your field and drive readers to your website, providing articles written by you to targeted online media can also drive traffic to your website, often with no out-of pocket expense. Just remember to include a short biography that outlines what you do and a link to your website at the bottom of each article you publish.

Permission-Based Email Marketing

Permission-based email marketing can be a low-cost and very effective component of your web marketing strategy. It can help to build a relationship between your business and target market, and can drive traffic back to your website. Email marketing can consist of direct email blasts and sales letters, personalised auto-responders, and/or email newsletters. If you have the budget and don't have the time, you can certainly hire a freelancer or a firm to conceptualise, develop and publish your email messages for you. Although, for many small businesses, the costs associated with fully managed solutions are simply too high. The advantage to email marketing is that you can choose a do-it-yourself option, where you do all of the work, or part of it yourself, saving hundreds, even thousands of dollars.

Self-Publishing in Low-Cost Internet Tools

There are a number of very easy to use self-publishing

solutions available to small businesses. The costs of these tools are low—from USD $20 per month and up—and they are usually offered at a monthly or per-1000 email rate. The solutions are hosted entirely online, allowing you access from any computer connected to the Internet. Further, they are designed for small business owners with little technical knowledge. At a minimum, they offer a database, where you can house and manage your email addresses, a selection of HTML templates for your email messages, the ability to import your own templates, plain-text options, testing functions, and added extras such as customisable auto-responders and forward-to-a-friend and unsubscribe features.

You may even find an email publishing tool designed specifically for your industry. For example, the real estate industry has a number of do-it-yourself and fully managed email newsletter solutions available, some of which even include "canned" articles that users can choose to include in their own newsletter.

Here are some popular self-publishing solutions to consider:

— Constant Contact - www.constantcontact.com.

— MyMailOut.com - www.mymailout.com.

— Topica - www.topica.com.

— Microsoft - www.microsoft.com/smallbusiness.

Problem with Spam

It must also be noted that more and more email marketers are struggling with spam filters, which are designed to protect email users from unscrupulous and unsolicited advertising. The problem arises when spam filters do such a good job that they succeed in filtering out legitimate marketing messages that email recipients have requested to receive. Unfortunately, as spam proliferates, as it undoubtedly will, the filters will only become better, causing email marketers to scramble to devise new ways to get their messages out to the public.

Ensuring High Delivery Rates

The easiest way to ensure that your emails will be delivered is to get permission from your client base to market to them through email. Getting permission is critical, particularly since new privacy legislation was introduced in 2004, which regulates how businesses collect, store and use their customers' personal information. This includes email addresses. Getting permission may mean asking in advance if you can send emails for a specific purpose, and requesting that your email address be flagged as legitimate in the recipient's list to ensure your messages bypass any filters s/he may have installed.

Currently, it also seems that HTML emails are becoming caught in spam filters more readily than plain-text emails. This may mean that a simple, plain-text email containing a link to an online message is the most effective method for getting your message out. Alternatively, you can test your email messages for deliverability using software such as SpamCheck which checks your emails' subject lines and body copy for filter triggers. to To learn more about email marketing visit www.emailsherpa.com.

Role of Business Blogs

A blog or weblog is simply a web page that scrolls chronologically like a journal and contains links to other websites of interest. Blogs, as creative online journals, have been used by technical specialists for a number of years, but business blogs, or b-blogs are just now making inroads into the mainstream. As an alternative, low-cost means of electronic communication, blogs can make up a significant part of your overall marketing strategy. Although b-blogs carry an inherent marketing focus not found in creative weblogs, their casual structure provides the opportunity to connect with readers on a more immediate and personal level than traditional websites and newsletters allow.

Affiliate programmes

Affiliate programmes, also known as referral programmes or partnership programmes, involve the use of affiliates to help market a website's products and services in return for a payment for each sale, lead, action, or visitor generated. Amazon.com has created one of the most sophisticated and successful affiliate programmes on the Internet—a programme that has no doubt contributed to their high level of brand recognition online, and the significant traffic and resulting revenue their site generates.

Costs to implement internet marketing

The costs to implement Internet marketing strategies can vary widely in the industry. They depend on the particular technique you choose, and the professional you choose to implement it. With a little reading, and a basic understanding of websites and the Internet, you may be able to implement some of these techniques on your own. Alternatively, you may find Internet marketing firms that charge "project rates" from $2,500 to $25,000. Therefore, it's very important to shop around. Also, keep in mind that most Internet marketing techniques require ongoing maintenance and these costs should be addressed in your marketing budget.

IMPORTANCE OF OFF-LINE MARKETING

Never underestimate the value of using low-cost, off-line marketing techniques to encourage people to visit your website. Ensure your website address is clearly listed on all of your marketing materials—that is, your business card, brochure, published articles, print advertisements, sandwich boards, your vehicle, and so on. And, don't be afraid to get creative with your off-line marketing strategies. Imaginative promotional techniques can be low-cost, yet attention getting ways to drive traffic to your website.

Developing a Plan

Marketing on the Internet doesn't consist of cookie-cutter strategies that work for everyone. For that reason, planning is an essential step in being successful online. Careful planning and monitoring will enable you to develop a strategy that fits your needs and budget, maps your progress, measures your return on investment (ROI), mitigates risk, and adapts as required.

When developing your plan, you'll want to consider the following important aspects:

— *Your buyers.* Who are they? What activities do they do online? Identifying your audience and their needs enables you to determine how best you can reach them online, thereby getting the most for your marketing dollar.

— *Your budget.* How much should you spend and, more importantly, how much do you have to spend? The amount you budget towards Internet marketing will depend on how integral the Internet is to your business success. Prioritise your needs based on your budget, projecting into the future and growing your plan as your revenues grow.

— *Your ability to support and maintain your plan.* Consider only implementing strategies you can handle. It is possible to do more damage than good to your business if you implement techniques for which you do not have the business processes or budget in place to support.

Importance of Measurement

Any professional marketer will tell you that it's not worth going to the effort of implementing an Internet marketing strategy, without also implementing a system to track your progress and determine what is working for your particular business. By tracking each strategy you implement, you will be able to measure your return on investment (ROI) and determine whether or not the strategy is effective.

Here's an easy way to track targeted campaigns. First, purchase a good statistics package to measure your website traffic. The statistics generated should tell you where your website visitors are coming from, where they are going, how long they are staying, and from which part of your site they are leaving. Then, use dedicated promotional codes for different campaigns that you test so that you can follow which campaigns are drawing customers to your site.

3

Online Marketing Strategies

When marketing and advertising on-line you have to choose a suitable on-line marketing strategy for you and your business. Choosing the correct on-line marketing strategy for your business is essential if you are going to get the most out of advertising and marketing your company on-line. There are many services to choose from for your companies on-line marketing strategy. These include cost per click, banner advertising, pay on page placement, Google SEO, search engine promotion and search engine optimization. There are so many advertising companies available to offer your company an on-line marketing strategy or internet marketing solutions. Here at Weblinx an on-line marketing company who can provide your business with an on-line marketing strategy which will best benefit your company when advertising on-line. Weblink.biz have many packages available for your internet marketing and are willing to provide you with advice for any on-line marketing strategy you wish to take from us.

Successful Marketing Strategies

The key to successful marketing is very simple: know your audience. Before you spend any time or money on marketing, you need to know who your target market is. What types of customers are most likely to buy the types of products you are selling? For example, males or females? What age bracket? What income bracket? Are you trying to reach people with certain interests or skills? Once you know the profile of your typical customer, you need to find ways of reaching customers with that demographic profile. This may involve on-line advertising, offline advertising, or a combination of the two. But don't even begin to think about spending money on marketing until you've spent time thinking about who you are trying to reach. You may even need to do some market research to uncover this information. Your marketing efforts won't be successful unless you are spending your marketing dollars in the right places.

BRAND NAME

One of the most important marketing assets that you have is the name of your on-line store. Give it careful consideration. You should pick a name that's easy to remember yet distinct from other similar names on the Internet. Closely related to the issue of picking a name is choosing a suitable domain name. The domain name is the part of your Web site address that appears after "www." For example, the domain name for the Office Depot is officedepot.com and the domain name for Eddie Bauer is eddiebauer.com. Office Depot's Web site is at www.officedepot.com and Eddie Bauer's Web site can be found at www.eddiebauer.com.

To avoid confusing your customers, you will want to have a domain name that is as close as possible to your organisation's name. This will also make it easier for customers to find your Web site. Finally, keep in mind that you don't have to have "www" in your Web address.

Some organisations have chosen to drop it entirely, e.g. CBS promotes itself simply as CBS.com.

In addition, you can, with the help of the technical folks who support your site, sometimes use words or characters in front of your actual domain name, and get an extra "identity hook" that might be unique enough to draw attention to your site. One such example of this is the Web site Beer.com, which gained some attention during the 2000 Olympics. It ran an ad that used the address mmm.beer.com—indeed, during the commercial, the graphic showed the "www" flipping over to become "mmm," as the announcer mimicked the "mmmm" or "tastes good" sound. There was a huge increase in traffic to the site.

It's important that both your brand name and your Web site address be as distinctive as possible to avoid confusion with other similar companies selling on the Internet. There are tens of thousands of merchants on the Internet all vying for attention, making it difficult for on-line merchants with similar names to get noticed. Even if the domain name you want is available, you should find out if similar names currently used by on-line stores might compete with yours. Many on-line merchants have found it necessary to change their names because their names were being confused with other similar names on the Internet.

When trying to come up with a name for your on-line store, consider getting a group of friends or colleagues together to brainstorm with you. Alternatively, you could hire a market research firm to hold focus groups with consumers. If you really want to have a domain name that someone else has already registered, you could approach the owner and if he/she is interested in selling the domain name to you. Many companies register domain names but never activate them. Even a company that is using a domain name may consider selling it to you for the right price. Finally, if you believe that someone else has registered a domain name that infringes on a trademark that you own, you can pursue legal action against the owner of the domain name in question.

Alternatively, an appeals process exists for domain names, and it might be possible for you to launch an appeal to if the other party can be forced to give up the name. To learn about this option, visit a domain name registrar, and read about the international domain name appeals process. You can also visit the ICANN Uniform Domain Name Dispute Resolution Policy site at www.icann.org/udrp/udrp.htm for more information.

Get a Domain Name

To get a domain name, you can go to any one of the accredited domain name registers on the Internet, including Register.com. You can get a complete list of accredited domain name registrars on the InterNIC Web site at www.internic.com. The list can be viewed alphabetically or by geographical location. You don't need to have a Web site in order to register a domain name and most registrars will hold your domain name for you until you are ready to activate it on your on-line store. Many browserbased storefront solutions allow you to set up a domain name for your on-line store when you are setting up your account. This removes the need for you to go directly to a domain name registrar.

Once you have registered a domain name, you want to make sure that no one is registering similar names, or taking out a trademark similar to your name. To automatically track your name, consider using a service like NameProtect. One of NameProtect's services will constantly monitor new US trademark applications and domain name registrations for you and flag any applications/registrations that are identical or very similar to your domain name. It's a great way to keep informed of any potential threats to your brand name. This service will also help you identify companies that may be trying to register your domain name as a trademark. This is a potentially serious situation as you could lose your domain name if a trademark similar to your brand name is granted to someone else.

Offline Marketing

Perhaps the most important piece of advice give you in this guide is this: Don't restrict your advertising and promotional efforts to the Web. On-line stores often rely too heavily on on-line advertising at the expense of more traditional advertising vehicles that may actually produce better results. Throughout this guide, number of different ways for you to promote your on-line store on the Web. But it's important not to get too dependent on on-line marketing for your success. Think about the types of customers you are trying to attract and what the best methods would be to reach those customers. Rather than spending your money advertising on the Web, you may find that a more effective strategy would be to place advertisements in a couple of well-targeted magazines.

Instead, the company did some marketing research and identified a number of magazines that appealed to the company's target market: outdoorsmen. Ads featuring the company's Web site address were then placed in those magazines. In fact, the bulk of Noggintop's marketing budget has been spent on offline ads. You shouldn't ignore traditional advertising vehicles. Think about how you can use both print and broadcast media to reach your target audience. Be realistic with your expectations. In years past, many Internet companies invested millions in television ads with often disappointing results. Many companies quickly learned that brands can't be built overnight. It can take years to build a successful and recognised brand name.

That being said, if you develop any print or broadcast advertising, make sure that your Web address is featured prominently in your ads. You may want to even consider purchasing advertising for the sole purpose of promoting your Web site. It is important to use your imagination when looking for ways to raise awareness of your Web site. Don't limit yourself to radio, television, and print media. Why not advertise your Web address in buses or subways, or on the transfers handed out by your local transit authority? How about on newspaper polybags? Or in movie theatres? Some organisations have even gone so far as to include their Internet addresses on bananas! The possibilities are endless.

Retail Store

If your business has a brick-and-mortar retail presence, use it to promote your on-line store aggressively. Include your Web site on your receipts, invoices, and shopping bags, and print it on your catalogs and sales literature. Make sure that your Web address is advertised prominently both within your store and outside if you can. Many retailers, unfortunately, don't leverage their retail presence in this way.

On-line Gift Certificates

Brick-and-mortar stores give out gift certificates, so why not on-line stores too? Consider offering an on-line gift certificate that your customers can give to a family member or a friend. Gift certificates purchased on-line make great last-minute gifts because they can be sent by e-mail to arrive almost instantly. The recipient can then visit the store's Web site and apply the gift certificate toward the purchase of any products offered by the store.

How does it work? On-line stores that offer this service let you pay with your credit card and the gift certificate is delivered to the recipient by e-mail as soon as the payment is authorised. The gift certificate is essentially an e-mail message with a number attached to it. The recipient can redeem the certificate on their next purchase at that on-line store. When the recipient proceeds to check out of the store, they will be asked to provide their certificate number. The value of the gift certificate will then be deducted from the total amount of the purchase. Electronic gift certificates not only make great gifts—they're a great way to drive new customers into your on-line store!

Cross-Selling Products

You should get in the habit of cross-selling products in your on-line store to increase sales. This means that where possible, product pages on your on-line store should feature accessories or complementary products that your customers may be interested in. For example, consider what Smith & Hawken has done in their on-line store. Whenever a customer views a product, complementary products are displayed on the right-hand side of the page. For example, a customer may select a bench. Smith & Hawken realises that customers who are interested in purchasing a bench may also be interested in purchasing a matching chair or table. That's why there is a section called "Also Look At:" where complementary products are displayed, including an armchair and table. As you might expect, if you look at the Web page advertising for the armchair, the bench is recommended as a complementary product.

Product Referral Services

Many people find out about Web sites through word of mouth. So make it easy for your customers to tell other shoppers about your on-line store. For example, as customers are browsing through your Web site, they may come across products that their friends, co-workers, or family members may be interested in. Or they may want to tell a friend or family member about a product they would like to receive as a gift. That is why you should make it easy for customers to refer friends and relatives directly to specific product pages on your site. For an excellent example of how this can be done, visit RadioShack's on-line store.

At the bottom of every product page on the site is a graphic that says, "e-mail this page to a friend." Customers who click on that icon will be taken to another Web page where they are asked to provide the name and e-mail address of a friend. The recipient will receive an e-mail message that invites them to visit RadioShack's on-line store. A referral mechanism like this is an effective way to bring more people into your Web site.

Successful Affiliate Programmes

Many on-line merchants have built successful affiliate programmes for their on-line stores. An affiliate programme involves paying owners of other Web sites a commission for referring customers to your on-line store. In other words, you reward other Web sites for sending new customers to you. The idea is to find Web sites with visitors who are likely to be interested in your products. To this end, Web site owners usually try to find merchants who sell products or services related to their own Web sites.

A Web site with movie reviews may try to affiliate with a merchant who sells movies, and a Web site devoted to golf may align itself with a Web site that sells sporting goods or athletic apparel. It's in a Web site owner's best interests to identify merchants with compatible products because it will increase the likelihood of making lots of sales. You could sign up travel agencies to your affiliate programme and invite them to create links from their Web sites to yours. You would then pay the travel agencies a commission on any book sales and/or leads you get from their customers.

On-line retailers with affiliate programmes compensate customers in different ways. Some merchants pay affiliates strictly for sales, while other merchants compensate affiliates simply for sending a potential customer their way. Other programmes may compensate affiliates if a person clicks on an advertisement, regardless of whether that person turns into a lead or ends up purchasing a product. This is called a pay-per-click programme. Affiliate programmes can be extremely powerful because they allow you to increase your revenues by having your brand name displayed on dozens if not hundreds of complementary Web sites. There are literally thousands of affiliate programmes on the Web. Web sites that sign up can earn a percentage of every sale for referring customers to Staples.com.

There is no cost for affiliates of Staples to sign up, but they must first agree to the programme's terms and conditions and then complete an on-line application form that requests information about their Web site. If a Web site is approved into the programme, Staples will provide the owner with a selection of Staples.com graphics that can be placed on the Web site and linked to Staples.com. Every time someone clicks on the link and proceeds to buy something from Staples.com, the Web site owner will be paid a commission. Staples.com says its affiliate programme has been a success, with over thirty thousand Web sites signing up since the programme was first created.

The commission that you offer your affiliates is up to you. Some firms, like Staples, offer a percentage of sales; other firms offer flat fees. Commission structures can range from less than 1 percent to as high as 50 percent. Flat-fee commissions. Affiliate programmes are popular because they're an inexpensive way of attracting customers to your Web site. In essence, you are getting other Web sites to market your online store for you. Moreover, it doesn't cost a lot to get such a programme underway. Best of all, you may only have to pay affiliates if they generate sales or leads for you.

Affiliate programmes do have a number of drawbacks, however. It can be a burden to keep track of all of your affiliates and process all of the commission checks. Keep in mind that the number of affiliates you have really has no direct bearing on how successful your programme will be. For example, even though Staples.com has over thirty thousand affiliates, what really counts is the number of affiliates that are sending significant amounts of business to Staples.com. A lot of online stores have found that many of the Web sites that sign up for their affiliate programmes bring in very little business. That is why when you are setting up an affiliate programme, your focus should not be on signing up as many Web sites as possible, but finding those Web sites that can generate the most sales for you. Obviously, it's hard to screen Web sites in advance but eventually you will discover which affiliates are valuable and which are immaterial to your business.

As you might imagine, setting up an affiliate programme can take a lot of time and effort, especially once you begin to sign up hundreds of affiliates. You need to screen applicants, track sales from each affiliate, prepare commission checks, and spend time on other administrative functions that take you away from running your online store. For this reason, many online retailers hire organisations called affiliate programme providers that specialise in running affiliate programmes on behalf of online stores.

The cost of using an affiliate programme provider varies depending on the affiliate provider. For example, some companies charge a one-time fee plus they receive a monthly commission based on a percentage of affiliate sales. Others may charge a one-time setup fee, an annual renewal fee, plus a percentage of your payout—the amount of money you pay your affiliates. Still others have no set up fee, or commission charge but have a flat monthly fee. Which affiliate programme provider is best? It all depends on what you are looking for. Services and programme features vary from one affiliate programme provider to the next, so make sure you carefully consider all your options before making a final decision.

One of the major benefits of using an affiliate programme provider is that these organisations will help you find Web sites that can begin linking to your online store immediately. If you're a small business with very little brand name recognition, how is anybody going to find your Web site to learn about your affiliate programme? Affiliate programme providers maintain a directory of participating online stores so that interested Web sites can quickly find merchants they want to work with.

If you're interested in setting up an affiliate programme for your online store, start by getting in contact with the various affiliate programme providers listed earlier in the guide. When comparing affiliate programme providers, think about the following questions:

— How much does the affiliate programme provider charge you to set up an affiliate programme? As explained earlier in the guide, affiliate programme providers have different pricing schemes, so make sure you understand how you will be charged. Also find out if there is a minimum escrow amount that you must give the affiliate programme provider.

— What types of affiliate programmes are offered? As noted earlier, there are three basic types of affiliate programmes that you should be familiar with:

  — pay-per-click programmes-you pay a Web site for referring a visitor to your online store regardless of whether a sale results or not

  — pay-per-lead programmes-you pay a Web site for referring a visitor to your Web site to fill out a form or perform another action that may lead to an online or offline sale

  — pay-per-sale-you pay a Web site for referring a visitor to your Web site who immediately buys a product or service

— What type of performance tracking is provided? How sophisticated is the performance tracking? What information do the performance reports contain? How frequently are the reports updated? Are the reports delivered by e-mail in addition to being available on the Web?

— How user-friendly is their affiliate management software? What account management features does their software offer? How easy is it for you to update or replace the ads being served by your affiliates?

— What tools exist for communicating with your affiliates, both through the affiliate programme provider's

Web site and by e-mail? Can you target certain affiliates with special offers?

— Who issues the commission payments to your affiliates? Do you have to, or will the affiliate programme provider do that for you?

— How does the affiliate programme provider guard against fraud? For example, what happens if the same person clicks on a link to your Web site 50 times—do you have to pay for that?

— Is there any flexibility with regard to payout rates? Can you customise payout rates for different affiliates or do you have to give the same commission structure to everyone?

— Does the affiliate programme provider offer any client services to assist you with the implementation of your affiliate programme, or are you expected to do it on your own? What technical support is available for both affiliates and merchants? Are any consulting services offered?

— How easy is it for Web site owners to join an affiliate programme and create links from their Web sites to yours? To get the answer to this question, you visit some of the leading affiliate programme providers' sites and try signing up with some of their merchants. By doing this, you'll get a first-hand look at how the process works from an affiliate's point of view.

— What types of link options are available for your affiliates?

— Does the affiliate programme provide support for e-mail-based affiliate programmes? For example, how easy is it for an affiliate to include links to your Web site in their e-mail messages to customers?

— How many affiliates are part of the company's network? What is the company doing to recruit new affiliates into their network?

If you decide to work with an affiliate programme provider, don't rely solely on its Web site to promote your programme. You should also promote it on your own Web site and get other Web sites excited about the possibility of joining your affiliate programme.

One final note about affiliate programmes: many merchants, in addition to running their own affiliate programmes, have become affiliates of other Web sites in order to generate some extra cash. If you are thinking about becoming an affiliate of another Web site, you proceed carefully. Having an advertisement for another company on your Web site can compromise your image and credibility. Sometimes, the mere presence of an advertisement on your site can make you look unprofessional to potential and existing clients, especially if it promotes products or services unrelated to your current line of business. Accepting advertising for another company is an implied endorsement for that organisation and its product or services. Make sure that you are prepared to make that type of public statement. Keep all of these factors in mind when considering whether to accept advertisements for other merchants on your Web site.

This advice may seem contradictory since the whole purpose of an affiliate programme is to get other Web sites to display advertisements for your company. Won't they look unprofessional by displaying advertisements for you? Maybe. When you create an affiliate programme, you have to keep in mind that you're inviting other companies to display your brand name on their Web sites and it's never a good idea to let another company take control of your brand name. Sometimes it's hard to control how your affiliates display your advertisements, and in what context. When launching an affiliate programme, make sure you carefully screen your affiliates. Permission Marketing

You may have heard the term "permission marketing" before. It refers to a method of online marketing where the merchant asks permission from online shoppers to market to them directly by e-mail. Permission marketing is also known as "opt-in e-mail." Permission marketing follows two main principles. First, you only market to those customers who have specifically told you that they are interested in receiving e-mail messages from you. Second, you must give away something in order to get a customer's e-mail address.

The easiest way to undertake permission marketing is by establishing a mailing list that customers can join. You can then use the mailing list to send out promotional messages to your customers. The trick is to give your customers an incentive to join your mailing list. They ran a contest on their home page for a "dream trip to Tahiti." Customers were invited to enter their e-mail address into a box on the screen.

Once a customer entered his/her e-mail address, a new page appeared inviting the customer to join Payless ShoeSource's mailing list. The contest was the "hook" to get customers to spend a few minutes filling out the form that is required to join the mailing list. Once customers joined the Payless mailing list, they were automatically entered into the vacation contest.

Keep in mind that if you are going to set up a mailing list for your customers, you should clearly tell your potential customers how they can leave the list, and about any other conditions that might apply to the list.

Search Engines and Web Directories

Many online shoppers use a search engine or a Web directory when they are trying to find something on the Internet. A search engine is a Web site that indexes the contents of millions of Web pages. A Web directory, on the other hand, organises Web sites by category so that they can be easily browsed by Internet users. Unlike search engines, directories are usually compiled by human beings.

In the following table, we've listed the names and addresses of the most popular search engines and Web directories. Making sure that your Web site is registered with all of these sites is one of the most important things you can do to draw traffic to your store. Why all of them? Your customers won't all be using the same search engine or Web directory. Some people use Excite, some use AltaVista, some use Lycos, etc. By registering with all the major search engines and Web directories, you have the best chance of being found by online shoppers regardless of what search engine or Web directory they are using.

Growth of Search Engine and Directory Databases

Before you submit your site to any search engine or Web directory, you need to understand how their databases are developed. A search engine database is significantly different from a directory database. Automated computer programmes called spiders develop search engine databases. These programmes scour the Internet indexing the full contents of the millions of Web pages they find. These databases are intended to help you find instances of words or phrases on Web sites, similar to a dictionary or book index.

Web directory databases, on the other hand, list Web sites that have been selected by human beings and organised into distinct categories. These databases are similar to the yellow pages, which organise businesses by topic, and are more useful when you are interested in a specific topic. The confusion comes from the fact that all the major search engine Web sites now have not only a search engine database, but also a directory database. Often when you do a search on such a Web site, the results that are returned include information from both databases. This is also true of Web directory sites, most of which have a search engine database in addition to the directory database.

Web Site to a Search Engine Database

When you launch a Web site, you want to make sure that it is included in the search engine databases of both search engine Web sites and directory Web sites. There is a good possibility that the spider programmes that these Web sites use will find your Web site, index it, and add it to the search engine's database. However, it could take months for these spiders to discover your site, if they ever do. For these reasons, it's generally a good idea to visit each search engine and directory Web site and manually submit your Web site for inclusion in their search engine databases.

Add Search Engine's Database

To add your Web site to a search engine, go to the particular search engine site and look for a link or button somewhere on the main page that says something like "Add Your Web Site", "Add a Page" or "Add URL". Click on the button or link, and you'll usually be directed to a Web page where you can fill out a form and submit your Web site.

Add a Web Directory's Search Engine Database

Web directory sites may have their own search engine spiders that develop their search engine database but quite often the Web directory partners with an existing search engine. Alliances are very common, so it is worth the time to find out who is partnered with whom and submit your Web site to all the relevant search engines. This will maximise the number of search engine databases you appear in.

Web Site to a Directory Database

First and foremost, make sure you register your Web site with the major directories that listed earlier in the guide, as well as with any other Web directories that pertain to your industry. Look for information on their home pages explaining how your can submit your Web site to their database. You generally have to decide what category and sub-category would best represent your site. In some cases you do not have a choice. Look through each Web directory's help section to make sure you understand what is required and how to go about properly registering your site. Second, visit the Web site of each of the major search engines, and determine who provides their Web directly listings. Then visit each of those Web directories and submit your Web site, if you haven't already done so.

Charge to submit

If the submission is free, it can take anywhere from a few weeks to a few months for your Web site to be added to the database, assuming that it is accepted for inclusion. There is the very real possibility that your Web site will never appear in the search engine's index. But don't let this discourage you! Submit your Web site anyway—you have nothing to lose. And don't hesitate to keep submitting it again over time. The problem is that the Internet is growing so rapidly that many of the search engine and Web directory sites can barely keep up with the massive increase in the number of pages and sites.

Not only that, but they complain that many Web sites, particularly adult-oriented ones, continually submit requests for them to check new sites. Hence, they have been falling behind in indexing new sites and pages.

The result is that many search engines and Web directories now charge you a fee to submit your Web site for inclusion in their respective databases. However, payment of these fees does not guarantee that your Web site will be included in the search engine or Web directory database. In some cases the fee may only guarantee that your Web site will be considered for inclusion. Check each search engine's and Web directory's help files for specific information.

You may be wondering whether it's a good idea to pay to have your Web site included in a search engine and/or Web directory. If a paid submission service is available, you use it. In some cases, it's the only way to get your Web site added to a search engine or Web directory. On those Web sites where both free and paid submission services are offered, you opt for the paid submission. Why? As noted earlier, with free submission, there is no guarantee that your Web site will ever make it into the search engine or Web directory. By paying, you guarantee that your Web site will at least be considered for the search engine or Web directory in a timely manner. If you use the free submission option, you could be waiting around forever!

Increasing Likelihood of Success

The process of submitting your site to search engines and Web directories, and might or might not manage to get listed. Particularly if you are paying a search engine or Web directory to be considered for inclusion in their site, you might want to know if there are ways to design your site so that it is more acceptable for inclusion. Look through the help files of search engines and Web directories to they provide any hints, tips, and other guidance for your site. Some have submission criteria you may need to follow. There are no hard and fast rules—it can be a very subjective process. Suffice it to say you can be judged on content, appearance, relevance of your site, and other factors.

Effective Marketing Tools

Working with search engines and Web directories can easily consume a lot of time, and many Web site owners wonder whether the effort is really justified. Internet users rely heavily on search engines and Web directories when they are looking for information on the Web, so it's definitely worth your time to ensure that your Web site is included in all the major search engine and Web directory sites. At the same time, caution you against going overboard and relying too much on search engines and directories to drive traffic to your Web site. Search engines and directories are just one part of the marketing mix. Your marketing activities should include using offline media such as radio, television, and print, as well as other techniques.

The use of Web site analysis tools such as WebTrends that can help you analyse which search engines and directories your customers are using to find you. These types of tools can help you understand how much traffic on your Web site originates from search engines and directories.

Search Engine Optimization

The beginning of this guide, there are billions of Web pages on the Internet and thousands upon thousands of online stores, all clamouring for attention. When you submit your Web site to a search engine, you typically don't have any control over where your Web site will show up in the site's results list when someone searches for your company name or a keyword related to your business. For example, suppose you open an online store selling pasta products. If someone goes to a search engine, and types in the word "pasta", you're not going to be very happy if your Web site shows up on the seventh page of results. Most people won't bother looking past the second or third page of results when they are doing a search on the Internet. In fact, many people won't even bother looking beyond the first page of results. This means that if your Web site doesn't show up in the top ten or so results for a specific search such as "pasta", the chances of your Web site being seen by Internet users diminishes considerably.

Hence, an important part of online marketing involves a process known as search engine optimization ensuring that your Web site receives prominent placement on all the major search engines. Ideally, you want your Web site to show up on the first page of results when a potential customer searches for a keyword related to your business.

Before go any further, you need to understand three things. First, there is no simple method or magical formula for achieving good rankings on search engines. Second, every search engine uses different ranking criteria. This is why the same search performed on different search engines will yield different results. It is also why your Web site may be ranked number one on one search engine but appear in the twentieth position on another. Third, search engines are constantly changing the algorithms they use to index Web sites, so your site's ranking on any given search engine may be in a continual state of flux. Most search engines provide some information on their Web sites to help you understand how they rank Web pages. Visit each search engine, read the help files, and try to accommodate as many of the suggestions as possible.

Reading help files will help you to understand what you need to do to get a good ranking for your Web site. That being said, there are some general tips offer to help you improve your Web site's ranking on various search engines:

Don't use graphics

When you create the front page of your Web site, make sure you include lots of text that accurately describes your business. When search engines index your Web site, they can read text, but they can't read images. If your home page consists of a bunch of graphics and very little text, it's difficult for the search engine to properly index your Web site. This means it will be hard for Internet users to find it when they are using a search engine to find products and services. We're not suggesting that you not use graphics on your home page. However, if you use graphics, make sure they are accompanied by lots of text.

Choose important keywords

Choose important keywords related to your business and make sure those keywords are strategically positioned on your Web site. Come up with two or three terms or phrases that might be the "hot" keywords that Internet users are most likely to search for. These important words should appear more frequently, in headings or in an introductory paragraph which has descriptive text that mentions these "hot" keywords. This doesn't mean that you should blatantly repeat the same words over and over again on your Web site. Rather, when building your Web site, think carefully about the words you are choosing to use on your home page. Make sure you integrate words and phrases into your Web site that you think Internet users will be searching for.

Use meta-tags

Meta-tags are pieces of code that you include in the HTML code of your Web site to influence the description that search engines give your Web site and to influence the words that search engines associate with your site. If a Web site is using meta tags, looking at the Web site's HTML code. If you are using the Netscape Web browser, you can look at a Web site's HTML code by choosing "View" from the list of options at the top of your browser, then select "Page Source" or "Document Source". If you are using Microsoft's Internet Explorer browser, select "View" from the menu bar, then "Source".

The information in a description meta-tag is used by the search engine to create a summary description of your Web site. When an Internet user is browsing through a list of search results on a search engine, the summary description from the meta tag is sometimes used to create the abstract that appears under the title of each Web page. Many Internet users rely on these abstracts to help them decide which Web sites to visit. It is therefore important that you create a site summary for your Web site that accurately and concisely reflects its purpose.

A keywords meta tag looks like this:

<META NAME="keywords" CONTENT="candles, candle holders, aromatherapy candles, floating candles, scented candles, illume, illuminate, candle lanterns, candle lamps, illuminations candles, essential oils, holders for candles, candle pillars, tapers, votive candles, tealight candles, candlesticks, sconces, candlescapes, online stores, incense, handmade candles, handcrafted candles, beeswax candles, gel candles"> A keywords meta-tag is essentially

just a list of keywords related to your business. Notice that each keyword in the list is separated by a comma. A keywords meta tag increases the likelihood that your Web site will appear higher on the results list whenever someone does a search using any of the words or phrases that appear in your tag.

When creating your keywords meta tag, you don't repeat the same keyword multiple times in order to try and increase your Web site's ranking. Some search engines have been known to lower a Web site's ranking in their index or remove the site altogether if they discover this type of abuse.

Meta tags in this guide because so many Web sites use them and because they are often cited as an important online marketing technique. However, the main problem with meta tags is that only some of the large search engines recognise them—many ignore them altogether. Furthermore, on search engines that do pay attention to meta tags, they are only one of several factors a search engine uses to rank your Web site for users' searches. Therefore, meta tags are not a panacea for getting your site to the top of a search engine's results list—they are just one of many things that you can do to improve your site's chances of being found on the Web. If you want to find out whether a particular search engine recognises meta tags, visit its Web site and read the online help files.

Depending on what type of storefront software you used to build your online store, you may or may not be allowed to modify the HTML code that makes up your Web site. In order to create and modify your meta tags, you will need to have access to the HTML code behind your Web site. Check with the company you are using to host your online store to see if this is possible. If you are not technically inclined or you're not familiar with HTML code, you may want to hire someone to create your meta tags for you.

— Give your Web site a descriptive title. Make sure that the title of your Web page describes your business rather than simply mentioning the name of your business. The title of your Web site is what appears at the very top of your Web browser's window—it is not what appears on the front page of your Web site.

  Many search engines pay special attention to the words in your Web site's title when they index your Web site. In other words, you may increase the likelihood of appearing higher up on a search engine's results list if the words in your title closely match what an Internet user is looking for. What you shouldn't do is create a title like: "Welcome to my Web site" or "Welcome to My Home Page". Titles like this are much too generic.

  Your Web site title is also important for another reason. The title of your Web site is often the title that an Internet user will see in a search engine's list of results. Creating a good descriptive title for your Web site is one way to make it stand out from the rest. Internet users are most likely to click on Web sites that have clear, descriptive titles. The title of your Web site is controlled by a line of HTML code in your Web site called the title tag. A title tag might look like this:

  <TITLE>Foot Locker: The Source for Athletic Footwear and Apparel</TITLE> You'll need to have access to your online store's HTML code in order to change or modify your Web site's title.

— Get other Web sites to link to you. Contrary to popular belief, many search engines look at factors other than what's on your Web site in order to figure out where to rank your site. Generally speaking, the more Web pages that link to your Web site, the more "popular" your Web site is, and the higher your Web site's ranking in the Google database.

Many Web site owners, sometimes in sheer desperation or frustration, have enlisted professional help to try and improve their rankings on search engines. The reason that search engine optimization firms are in such demand is explained well by one of many companies that specialises in search optimization: "...Over the years the search engines and directories have gotten smarter and keep changing to the point where to work very hard to keep up to date on what techniques work best. Search engine optimization has become a very complex, sophisticated practice that requires constant research, practice, and re-evaluation to be effective."

Search engine optimization has become a popular business in recent years. There are also many small organisations that offer search engine optimisation services. Many Web design and online advertising firms have also entered this market.

Search engine optimisation firms use a variety of practices to improve Web site rankings for their clients, practices that are beyond the scope of this guide. If you're thinking of hiring a SEO firm, evaluate your options carefully. While many search engine optimisation companies do honest, legitimate work, there are just as many companies that use unethical techniques and are looking for a way to earn a fast buck. If one company, for example, that was duped out of over $2,000 after hiring a company that promised to get it listed in the top ten rankings of all the major search engines. The rankings never materialised, and the company never saw its money again. If the company you hire uses unacceptable techniques to boost your search engine ratings, you could wind up having your Web site banned from a search engine forever.

Search engine optimization is such a complicated business that it's hard to know what techniques a company is using. Even if they're explained to you, you may not understand, and this of course makes it difficult for you to figure out whether a certain practice is ethical or unethical. Before choosing a SEO company to work with, check references and ask to see the company's client list. This will help you to ensure that you are only dealing with legitimate companies that use industry-accepted practices.

Online Shopping Directories

Most of the major search engines and Web directories have shopping areas on their Web sites that showcase selected merchants and that list hundreds of merchants by product category. Many Internet users use one of these shopping directories when looking for online merchants to buy from, so it's a good way to get exposure for your online store. However, to get included in a search engine or Web directory's shopping directory, or to become one of its "featured stores" or "premier merchants", you usually need to be an advertising partner or be using the site's online storefront software. To become an advertiser, you will need to get in contact with the search engine or directory's advertising department for details about pricing.

It is important to point out that these types of advertising opportunities are often targeted are larger, established retailers as opposed to small businesses, so depending on your advertising budget and the size/profile of your business, you may find that this type of advertising opportunity is not practical or affordable.

POPULAR ONLINE ADVERTISING AND SPONSORSHIPS

One of the most popular online marketing strategies is to advertise on or sponsor other Web sites that attract the types of people who may be interested in buying your products and services. Suppose, for example, you sell luggage products. Why not advertise your online store on Web sites that attract travelers? Most Web sites that accept advertising have a section somewhere on the site that provides contact information for advertising inquiries as well as a general overview of advertising and sponsorship opportunities.

Before choosing to advertise on or sponsor any Web site, make sure that the site is reputable. You don't want to advertise on any Web site with a doubtful reputation or poor credibility. You should also obtain audited statistics that tell you how many visitors the site receives on a daily, weekly, and monthly basis. Also try to obtain as much demographic information as you can—data that will tell you what types of people the site attracts, including average age, income, and spending habits. You want to ensure that the Web site is attracting the same types of people who buy your products; otherwise your advertising dollars are being wasted. You should also find out what types of advertising or sponsorship packages are available and how much they cost. Will the Web site let you track how well your ad is performing? How frequently can you access usage statistics?

Form of Banner Advertisements

Online advertisements come in all different sizes and shapes, just like newspaper ads. However, online advertising often appears in the form of a banner ad. A banner ad is a small rectangular graphic that can either be animated or static. You can design it yourself, or have someone design it on your behalf—it's basically a small Web page or graphic. People can click on a banner ad to be immediately connected to the advertiser's Web site.

Banner advertisements are usually sold on the basis of page views, and page views are usually purchased on a cost per thousand (CPM) basis. For example, if you are told by a Web site that the cost of banner advertising is $60 per CPM, this means that you pay $60 for every thousand page views. This might represent a thousand people looking at that page—or it might mean five hundred people looking at that page two times each. There are hundreds of thousands of Web sites on the Internet that accept banner advertising. The key is to find Web sites that attract the types of customers you are interested in reaching. There is no sense buying banner advertising on a Web site if its visitors aren't in your target market.

The average price for a banner is between $5 and $50 per CPM, although rates can be much higher or lower depending on the Web site. The cost of a banner ad may also be influenced by the length of the contract you sign and where on the Web site the banner ad will appear. As you might expect, banner advertising on hightraffic sites like Yahoo! is typically more expensive than the industry average. The cost could also be affected by the way that the site charges for advertisements. It could be based upon the number of "impressions" or instead, it might be based upon the number of "click-throughs".

When purchasing banner advertising, you may come across terms like "run of category", "run of site", "run of network" and "fixed category", especially if you are inquiring about advertising on a search engine or Web directory. "Run of category" means that your banner advertisement will be rotated throughout a specific category area on the site, "run of site" means that your banner ad will be rotated throughout the entire Web site, and "run of network" means that your banner ad will be rotated throughout a network of other Web sites that are somehow related to the site you are advertising on. "Fixed category" advertising allows you to display your banner ad on the same page within a category all the time.

Creating Banner Advertising Campaign

Larger Web sites may require a minimum advertising buy of several thousand dollars. For a small business, this can be prohibitive. An alternative to purchasing banner ads through one of the big search engines and directories is to use a service like Microsoft's Small Business Centre where small businesses can create their own banner advertising campaigns and place them on select Web sites for a smaller up-front investment.

Professional Help in Online Advertising

If you want professional help with online advertising, you may want to consider using an advertising network to help you develop an online advertising campaign and target it at the right audience. Advertising networks typically use sophisticated profiling technology to target your ads at Internet users who would be most interested in the types of products or services you are selling. DoubleClick is an example of such a firm.

Effective Banner Ads

Many online shoppers say that they ignore them. Indeed, only 3.2 percent of online advertisers surveyed by Forrester Research said that banner ads were effective in driving traffic to their Web sites. The other problem is that most

Web users who see banner advertisements don't click on them. In fact, the average click-through rate for banner ads is less than 1 percent. In other words, no more than 1 percent of all the Web users who see banner ads on the Internet actually click on them. That's an even lower response rate than using direct mail! But such a dismal click-through rate doesn't mean that banner ads are ineffective. Some companies run banner advertising campaigns with the goal of increasing brand awareness. If this is the goal of your online advertising campaign, the number of click-throughs isn't as important as the number of people who see your banner ad.

Keyword-Based Advertising

Many Web sites, including many of the major search engines and Web directories, offer keyword based advertising. Here's how it works. You purchase one or more words and/or phrases related to your business. When a customer searches for any of those words, an advertisement for your Web site will appear. The advertisement may be a banner ad or another type of online advertisement that you create. For example, suppose your own a business that sells pools and spas. You could purchase the word "pools" on Yahoo! so that whenever someone searches for that word, a banner ad for your company will appear on the search results screen.

Keyword Based Marketing

Part of the challenge in using keyword-based marketing on the Internet is to pick the keywords that your customers are most likely to be using when they are doing searches on search engines and Web directories. This will likely require a bit of brainstorming on the part of yourself and your staff. That's your job. To help you brainstorm, you might want to check out a few of the search engines that reveal what Internet users are searching for. For example, Lycos has a service called "The Lycos 50 Daily Report" that shows you what people are searching for on the Lycos search engine. Every week, Lycos publishes the 50 most popular searches from the past week.

One of the least expensive online marketing techniques, but perhaps one of the most effective, is getting links from other Web sites. Contact suppliers and manufacturers you work with to see if they will link from their Web sites to yours. Why is this important? Customers often visit the Web sites of manufacturers or suppliers when they are researching a purchase. If the manufacturer provides a link from their Web site to yours, the customer may end up making the purchase online from you. This manufacturer benefits from the sale as well, given that you are selling more product, so it's in the manufacturer's best interest to link to you. You should also contact any industry associations you belong to and ask if they will link to you. The idea is to try and get as many Web sites to link to you as possible. As noted earlier, this can even help you with your placement on search engines since many search engines take a site's links into account when they decide where to rank it.

Once you invest in an online store, you owe it to yourself to monitor how well your investment is paying off. The number of sales you receive is only part of the picture. You also want to be able to track the number of people who visit your online store, where they come from, and which search engines and directories they use to find you. This information is vital to your business because it will help you assess whether your marketing activities—both online and offline—are succeeding or failing. If you don't already receive daily traffic statistics from your Internet service provider, Web hosting service, or online store service, or if the reports you receive don't provide enough detail, consider signing up for one of many the third-party Web site analysis services.

Two thirds of all online shoppers abandon their shopping carts before making a purchase. A software programme like the ones listed above can help you analyse what path customers are taking through your site and what the most popular "exit pages" are so that you can minimise customer abandonment. One powerful Web site tracking programme is WebTrends. Webtrends has a number of different versions of its programme that will allow you to track sales activity on your Web site. WebTrends is capable of generating very detailed sales reports for your Web site.

Most Web site analysis programmes work over the Web so you don't need to install or configure any software. You simply cut and paste some code into your Web site, and the service will start to track your Web site immediately. You'll be given a password and username, and you can log into the vendor's Web site at any time to access your reports. In some cases, you may have the option of purchasing Web site analysis software and installing it on your computer.

Users of WebTrends, for example, can choose between browser-based versions that provide real-time statistics over the Web and software versions that can be installed on your computer and integrated with internal databases. Several versions of WebTrends software are available depending on your reporting needs and the complexity of your Web site. If you decide to go with a software solution, you will need to have access to the Web servers of the company that hosts your online store. Check with the company hosting your online store to find out if you can use WebTrends. A free 14-day trial version of WebTrends can be downloaded at www.webtrends.com.

When evaluating a Web site analysis programme, don't buy strictly on the basis of price. Examine the types of reports you are getting from two perspectives. First, how easy are the reports to read and understand? Secondly, what type of reports are available and how much detail is provided? In particular, find out if the programme will allow you to do any type of advanced e-commerce tracking, such as tracking sales or the performance of your advertising campaigns. Most of the entry-level Web site analysis programmes do not provide this type of e-commerce tracking. If you are interesting in tracking orders on your Web site and monitoring sales activity for all the products in your online store, you should be prepared to spend significantly more for a product that has these capabilities.

4

Internet Marketing Strategy

Explore strategies and techniques that you can use on the Internet that will enhance and support your business's overall marketing objectives. Learn how to conduct banner promotions, generate targeted online traffic, positioning your content, and over all brand awareness.

Myths of Internet Marketing

Like a worm swallowing its tail, the Internet marketing beast feeds mostly on itself. The vast majority of what appears on the Internet about marketing is designed to help you market products and services sold and delivered exclusively on the Internet. So what does that mean for the independent professional whose web presence is primarily aimed at selling his or her own personal services? You know, services delivered the old-fashioned way, by humans interacting face-to-face or at least voice-to-voice. At best, the average professional is likely to be overwhelmed by the sheer volume of Internet marketing advice available. At worst, he or she is being seriously misled by it.

The problem is that marketing your own professional services is simply not the same as marketing a retail product or an anonymous business service.

You can't sell corporate consulting like you do web hosting; nor can you sell life coaching the same way you do an e-book. If you try to market yourself by following advice designed for marketing Internet products and services, you're likely to make some serious mistakes.

Here are five Internet marketing myths that may be hazardous to the health of your business.

Myth 1 - It all starts with a Great Web Site

Actually, the place where it starts is with a well-defined service. If you don't have a crystal clear picture of who you are marketing to and exactly what you're selling them, the best web site in the world won't get you clients. Before you even think about building a web site, you should know who your target market is, how to describe your professional specialty, and what specific benefits your work provides for your clients.

The content of your site is much more important than the design. Yes, you should have a professional-looking site, but a brilliant design and dazzling graphics won't pay off anywhere near as well as a clear explanation of why a client should work with you. Useful material such as articles, assessments, and other samples of your expertise will go much further to persuade prospective clients than flash intros and interactive menus.

Myth 2 - More Traffic Translates to Increased Profits

The only result that more traffic to your web site guarantees you is increased bandwidth use by your web host. Before spending money on banner ads, web directories, or pay-per-click listings to drive more visitors to your site, you need to be sure that they'll want to do business with you once they get there.

Ask your colleagues and current clients to critique your site. Do they understand what you are offering? Can they see concrete benefits to your target audience? Revise your site based on their feedback. Then personally invite some prospective clients to visit and touch base afterward. Do your prospects seem more inclined to do business with you after seeing your site? If so, you're on the right track. If not, you still have more work to do.

Myth 3 - Do Whatever it Takes to Build Your List

There's no question that a substantial opt-in mailing list is a valuable marketing asset, but the quality of names on your list is much more important than the quantity. Acquiring names through giveaways of other people's material, trading lists with joint venture partners, or purchasing them from a vendor rarely provides qualified buyers truly interested in your services.

Absolutely, ask your site visitors and people you meet to join your mailing list and offer them something of value in return. A well-written ezine, helpful report, or informative audio are all effective premiums. But, your premium should be directly related to the services you provide and also serve to increase your professional credibility. Names acquired from promotional gimmicks or unknown sources seldom turn into paying clients.

Myth 4 - Killer Copy is the Secret to Sales

Hype-laden web copy may be effective in selling certain info-products or courses, but it hardly inspires trust. You're not going to convince anyone to hire you individually as a consultant, coach, trainer, designer, or financial advisor by offering "not one, not two, but three valuable bonuses" as if you were selling steak knives on late-night TV.

Your Internet marketing persona should reflect the same professionalism as the work you do with your clients. If writing marketing materials isn't your forte, by all means hire a professional copywriter. But be sure you hire one with experience writing for professionals like yourself. The copy on your web site should inspire feelings of confidence about your abilities, and communicate your reliability and solid qualifications.

Myth 5 - Just follow the Winning Formula and you will get Rich

There's only one surefire recipe for Internet wealth, and that's the business of selling surefire recipes. There seems to be an infinite number of buyers for every new get-rich-on-the-net scheme that is invented, but paradoxically, a precious few people actually making money on the web.

The Internet may be a different medium for marketing professional services than making calls, writing letters, or speaking to people in person, but the same time-honored principles still apply. There is no new winning formula. The secret to landing clients is what it always has been — build relationships and get people to know, like, and trust you.

If your web site, ezine, and other Internet-based activities contribute to building long-term, trusting relationships with prospective clients and referral sources, you'll get business on the web. But if you blast your message out to anyone who will listen, aiming for a quick profit, the Internet won't bring you any more business than standing on a street corner with a megaphone.

Web Technology in Marketing

Every independent professional should have a web site, an ezine, and an email marketing strategy, right? If you're not taking maximum advantage of web technology to market your professional services, you are behind the times, and missing out on huge opportunities. At least that's what most marketing experts would have you believe. But how valid is this advice? And is it for everyone?

Before email was widely available, marketing newsletters were printed on paper and sent by mail. There's no question that e-mail is a more economical solution for sending a newsletter. Instead of being able to afford only a few hundred newsletters at a cost of $1 or more each, you can send tens of thousands for only pennies. With an ezine, technology can save you money and allow you to extend your marketing reach.

This is one of the many ways that web technology can be your friend. Here are some others:

— A web site can attract new customers to your business from across the street or far outside your local area. If your site has high rankings in the search engines under appropriate categories, or many links from keywords prospective clients might search for, you may get dozens of inquiries from people who otherwise would never hear of you.

— Using email autoresponders can help you automate your follow-up with likely prospects. Just subscribe a prospect to an autoresponder list once, then send periodic broadcasts to the whole list, encouraging prospects to hire you or attend your learning programs.

— Participating in online discussion lists and message boards can allow you to network with a large group of people in your target market without leaving your home or office. Appearing on live chats or webinars permits you to be a public speaker without the time and expense of travel, and speak to national or global audiences.

For these reasons and more, it appears that using web technology is an affordable way to reach prospective clients easily. You can potentially attract larger numbers of prospects for fewer dollars than with many more traditional methods of outreach. But there are pitfalls.

Broadcast email can be an efficient solution for following up with prospects who already know about you. But it's a terrible way to introduce yourself to a prospect for the first time. Far too many coaches, consultants, trainers, and other professionals add subscribers to their ezine or autoresponder lists without their permission. Not only is this ineffective as a marketing strategy since most readers simply delete e-mail from people they don't recognize, but it can seriously backfire when someone is offended by your unsolicited mail.

Here are some other ways that using technology in marketing can become your foe:

— Technology makes it easy to hide. When you have a web presence, an ezine, and use e-mail autoresponders to contact your customers, you may think there's no reason to contact them in person. You may feel justified in not picking up the phone, attending a business event, or suggesting a lunch date if you think your technology is doing the job for you. But a web site or e-mail isn't an equal substitute for a prospect hearing your voice or seeing your face. It's pretty rare for someone to hire a professional without talking to him or her first, so if you put off the talking, you may also be putting off the hiring.

— Launching and maintaining an attractive and useful website, and achieving high search engine rankings for it, can be an expensive and time-consuming project. Unless you pay close attention to your budget, you can easily find yourself spending much more to land each client than you would ever pay using offline marketing methods. A high-traffic web site is a valuable resource for a business that can take advantage of a global presence or a large volume of new clients. But if your business is primarily local or you only need a few new clients each year, you may end up paying for a level of visibility you don't really need.

— Too many inquiries from the web can waste your time. Anonymous visitors to your site will often email to ask about prices and other details. These inquiries are completely unqualified — you don't know anything about the people who are writing. If you take the time for a thorough reply to each one, they can consume a significant amount of energy. On the web as well as off, prospects who are referred to you by people who know your work are much more likely to hire you than those who find you by accident. If that's so, perhaps it makes sense to put more effort into building referrals than into building a broader web presence.

Web technology is really no different than any other method of marketing your services in that you must judge the appropriateness of each strategy for your unique circumstances. If you find writing to be a chore, perhaps a regular ezine is not the best choice for you. If you only need a few large, local clients each year, you may want a web site for prospects to explore after you contact them, but not spend your money on web directory listings or search engine optimization. Autoresponder reminders may be effective to increase enrollment in public workshops, but not such a good idea to sell in-house training to corporations.

Just because a strategy is the latest and greatest doesn't mean it's the best. Publishing a blog may be terrific if your target market spends a lot of time online, but not so good to reach those who rarely open their browser. Webinars can be an effective tool for attracting high-tech or corporate clients, but not for home business owners or consumers who operate older, slower computers with dial-up Internet access.

Relying completely on technology to bring in clients can also give you a false sense of productivity. When you are writing copy for your web site or setting up autoresponders, you feel like you are taking action about marketing. And these activities can be important behind the scenes steps, but you shouldn't confuse them with direct outreach to prospective clients. Web copy won't make any sales until people see it, and autoresponders will have no effect until people are subscribed to them.

Web technology provides just another set of marketing tools, not a complete solution. Using every marketing tool the web has to offer is not a requirement of doing business. The purpose of your marketing should be to bring you enough clients to earn the level of profit you desire. When marketing technology adds to your bottom line, it's worth employing. When it doesn't, there's no reason to use it.

Online Retailers

Are you operating a small or medium-sized online retail store? Have your ecommerce efforts been thwarted by a big online retailer? If so, take heart! Things aren't as bad as they might seem. In fact, instead of being intimidated by the big online retailers – you should welcome the opportunity to compete with them! Here are some things that they won't tell you that could give you a real advantage when trying to gain more ecommerce customers at their expense. Here are some of the things that the big online retailers don't want smaller competitors to know that they're saying behind your back:

> "We're concerned that you can look just as big as us online" Think about it – for all the time, money, resources, and energies that go into the website of a large online retailing operation – they still have most of their traffic landing on their home page.

It's the same with you, the small online retailer. When a potential online buyer looks at your home page, they can easily think that you are much larger than you really are. How do you tell the difference between a one-person operation, a ten-person operation, or a large retail site? It's hard – even for professionals. One key point here: make sure that your home page design and layout measure up to the current standards of professionalism in the industry today.

"You might be better at reaching a niche audience"

Giant online retailers need to reach giant audiences in order to achieve their sales goals. For the most part they aren't even interested in a smaller niche audience. Large online retailers are looking for search terms and advertising buys that will attract the largest possible pool of potential buyers to their site. You, on the other hand, can be far more selective in your choice of products offered, keywords targeted, and where you choose to advertise. In addition, you can select target audiences who may purchase more expensive products in smaller volumes, or who will be much more loyal buyers and repeat purchasers.

"We can't deliver personalized service like you can"

Similarly, the larger the company, the harder it is to give truly outstanding and personalized service. As a small online retailer, you can actually get to know your customers. In fact – you must get to know your customers in order to keep them from straying to a larger competitor with lower prices on the same items. There are so many different and unique ways to really embrace your buyers! Here are a few: send an extra special little gift each time someone buys; collect your buyers birth dates and send them a birthday present on that special day; keep their information in a special place so that when they contact you they get a personal response in the fastest possible time; note buyer preferences and send them a personalized note informing them of new products that are of interest to them. You can think up many more ways to give personalized service for your site if you spend some time pondering it.

"You can rank higher in key search engines than us"

Some large retailers have a great search engine marketing and search engine optimization strategy – many do not. A great leveler of the playing field with regard to online buyers is your search engine presence. You will gain market share at the expense of the large online retailers if you rank higher than they do on key search terms at key search engines. Make certain that you understand and implement professional search engine marketing strategies. Study search engine optimization techniques. Understand paid inclusion programs. Gain expertise in pay per click marketing engines such as Google AdWords and Overture. When buyers use search engines to look for your products and services make certain that your results are visible – whether in paid or organic listings.

"Our online operations are a neglected step-child in our company"

A huge advantage that the smaller online retailer holds is simply the focus on the business and the commitment to success. Most online retailers were 'bricks-and-mortar' players long before their forays into the online space. Therefore, all of their operations were originally developed for an offline world. Further, the original 'bricks-and-mortar' component of the company may actually be jealous of the fast growth and success of the online retailing component – leading to internal bickering and power struggles. One thing is for certain: both the small online retailer and the larger online retailer have had approximately the same amount of time to develop experience in online selling. Purchasing via the Internet is still relatively new – and there are many differences between selling in a physical store and selling in a virtual environment.

The small retailer can work these differences to their advantage. So even a prestigious and long established offline retailer may actually be playing catch-up when it comes to online retail.

Action items for the smaller online retailer

To compete against larger retailers keep the following competitive tactics in mind. Develop a professional web site and make it look just as inviting as the big player's sites. Consider focusing on a specialized or niche audience that is likely to be overlooked by larger retailers – simply because the market is perceived to be too small. Differentiate by offering superior, personalized service. Make your customers so happy that they begin to talk about you to others. Master search engine optimization and search engine marketing techniques – or hire professionals to help you achieve top search engine rankings. Embrace online operations and take advantage of the all the possibilities that the Internet offers to increase your sales. Good luck with your online ecommerce ventures!

Marketing in Virtual World

Before the Internet, small business owners like yourself were usually limited to a local market -resorting to expensive advertising and brochures, direct mail, cold-calling, networking at the local Chamber of Commerce or Rotary. You hoped customers found you through word-of- mouth or a Yellow Pages ad. Today, you can work with a consultant, a financial planner, or a business coach across the country as easily as someone across town. In the Internet age, prospects often find you (instead of the other way around).

This is the age of the virtual customer. Yet, although the Internet has made it perfectly reasonable to land a major client you've never met in-person, it has also created new expectations among consumers.

Prospects now "Google" around to find someone with your skills. They expect you to make a good virtual "case" for yourself. If you don't pass the test, or make a bad impression, or appear lackluster compared to your competitors, you will lose the potential client. The only way to be truly successful in business is by establishing a good reputation. And understanding the way business has shifted in the Internet age can help you bring the potential of marketing your business into the virtual world.

The Internet has increased the expectation among consumers that businesses will have a credible online presence. Many of us now form "first impressions" of people and companies via our Internet browsers. From the moment your name and business appear in a Web browser to the moment your Web site loads, your first impression often means the difference between a shot at your prospect's business, or being shut out. Think about it. You have probably used the Internet to research a company or a person you're considering doing business with. Certainly potential clients and customers are checking you out online, too.

Prospects you've never met are forming opinions about your business at the click of a mouse. Internet first impressions are not just influenced by how your Web site looks, but also by how often your business appears or how high it ranks in a web browser.

We all know people who command rapt attention whenever they speak. Others want to listen to, learn from, and emulate them. They are centers of influence, a distinction you can pursue online by developing the following qualities:

— Share inside knowledge with your target market;

— Participate, listen, contemplate, and offer thoughtful responses;

— Be willing to voice an opinion;

— Assume leadership positions in your industry

Certainly, experience counts. But this is not the only prerequisite to becoming an online center of influence that will earn you the distinction of 'trusted advisor' within your target market.

Start by making your Web site a resource for your industry. Feature lots of useful information, including articles, links, downloadable files, customer resources, and anything else of use to your target market. Be generous and give, give, give!

Virtual Podium with Teleclasses

Teleclasses are a great way for businesses to develop a virtual reputation. They can be promoted easily by email, and provide information to prospects, clients, and customers all over the world, with minimal cost and effort.

Business coach and teleclass leader Michael Losier set up a teleclass about exhibiting at trade shows: 'I had 60 students in my first class, which was very profitable, and many later hired me as a consultant." Also, it may be just as effective and less effort to participate as a guest lecturer in another professional's class rather than producing your own teleclass.

Online Articles

Online articles draw upon your expertise by providing useful information that Web site visitors are actively seeking out. Online articles position you as an expert in your field and convey a level of authority that establishes trust and sets the stage for sales. When high-traffic, high-credibility Web sites and newsletters publish your articles, you ride on the coattails of their loyal relationships with readers. Your articles are seen by visitors as referrals from trusted friends.

Some of the most prime "real estate" in the world these days is at the top of the search engine listings. The most widely used search engines rank Web sites by the quantity of other Web sites that link to them. This means that every article you publish that links to your Web site can improve your search engine rankings.

Creating Online Relationships

Most business networking used to happen when we recommended an associate, swapped business cards, or connected with colleagues over lunch. But increasingly, social networking is migrating to the Internet. Through social networking Web sites and online discussion lists, entrepreneurs can access virtual communities of prospects and associates while developing virtual "platforms" to generate leads and sales and establish themselves as recognized experts.

Marketing consultant Max Blumberg credits his involvement in Ecademy.com, a business networking Web site, with elevating his business profile and generating new clients. "When I first encountered Ecademy I'd never heard of online networking, but the benefits of a large community where I could share ideas and cultivate new relationships was very appealing."

Blumberg started by posting a profile about his business, then started sharing his knowledge with other Ecademists. "I set up a club where members could get help with common marketing challenges. Many of these people became clients and friends with whom I socialize. We reciprocally use each other's services," says Blumberg, whose Ecademy presence has even been noticed by large companies who are starting to contact him.

The key to building a niche community is identifying your ideal customers and the communities they belong to. By targeting the best, most favorably inclined prospects within a niche, you can become your target market's vendor of choice, and sell more with far less effort.

Networking on the Internet

Networking is one of the most effective ways to find clients for any consulting or professional services business. But if you limit your networking to only what you can do in person, you'll be missing out on a huge number of possibilities. Networking is more than entering a room full of people and exchanging business cards. It's creating a pool of contacts with whom you can exchange clients, referrals, resources, ideas, and information. Networking can happen by phone, by mail, over coffee, and increasingly, over the Internet.

The growth of the Internet has created many new ways to network without ever leaving your home or office.

Pick a topic, any topic, and there will be multiple web sites and online communities devoted to it. Almost any type of Internet presence offers opportunities for networking. In your favorite search engine, type the name of your profession or specialty, e.g. "interior design" or "marketing communications." Or, if you have a clearly defined target market, you can use that, e.g. "baby boomers" or "biotechnology." Skip the sponsored links or banner ads and focus on the detailed results. What you will find is the following:

— *Professional Associations & Schools* — Many association or school sites provide member rosters, resource pages, back issues of newsletters, event calendars, and bulletin boards or discussion lists. Not all of these features will be restricted to members or students.

— *Resource Sites & Online Communities* — These include directories of people in the profession, vendors, articles, event calendars, bulletin boards, discussion lists, live chats, and links to even more resource sites.

— *Publications* — Magazines and newsletters maintain sites that offer everything from back issues to complete online communities.

— *Job Postings* — These may appear on any of the above sites, and often include opportunities for independent professionals, not just those looking for full-time employment.

— *Colleagues & Competitors* — Colleagues and competitors may be exactly the same people, depending on your relationship with them. Their sites will tell you more about them and their work, and may offer many of the same features as resource sites.

— *Potential Clients* — Their sites will tell you about the work they do, current and upcoming projects, and even the names of executives and managers.

Also, if you subscribe to an online service offering interactive "channels," like America Online, CompuServe or MSN, there may be an entire area dedicated to your profession or target market. Some of these resources are available to non-members as well. Now, how can you use all this information to network? Here are some of the most common ways:

— *Bulletin Boards* — These are web pages where you can view and post questions and comments on a specific subject. Answering a posted question is an excellent way to demonstrate your expertise, become known to the people who frequent the board, and get to know others in your field.

— *Discussion Lists* — These are like bulletin boards, but are e-mailed to members of the list daily, weekly, or whenever a new posting arrives. When posting to these lists, you can include more information about yourself in a signature box at the end of each e-mail. Keep it short, but include some reason for people to get in touch with you outside the list, such as, "Subscribe to my free newsletter," or, "Visit my web site for a free resource guide." In addition to locating discussion lists through search engines as described above, you can find them through online community hosts such as Yahoo Groups or MSN Groups.

— *Live Chats* — Many online communities sponsor real-time chats on specific topics. Participating in these chats is an excellent way to meet people interested in the subject being discussed. Chat rooms that require membership are best, because you are more likely to encounter professionals seriously interested in the topic instead of people just looking for a date. Attending chats featuring a guest speaker can be more valuable than you might think. If you ask a question during one of these, don't be surprised if people contact you by e-mail during or after the chat to offer you more resources related to your question. You can make exactly the same type of contacts when you are the one who has something to offer.

— *Articles* — Notice who is writing them and who is being written about. These people are likely to be leaders in your field, or at least highly visible. That makes them good contacts for you. Send them an e-mail complimenting them on the article and suggesting you get acquainted for mutual benefit. Make a specific suggestion about what you can offer, e.g. referrals or resources.

— *Others in Your Field* — These may be colleagues, competitors, vendors, or potential clients. Approach them collegially with ideas about how a relationship could benefit you both, such as exchanging referrals, pooling resources, links on each other's web site, or trading endorsements or articles in each other's ezine.

If you can't find a board, list, chat, or site with the exact focus you want, consider starting one of your own. While hosting one of these communities takes time and effort, it will also put you in the center of the network that forms around it instead of on the outskirts.

Levels of Internet Marketing and the Sales Process

You can provide human interaction to potential Internet clients and customers so that you are able to move that client or customer through a successful sales process, but how?

You do this by following a five step process in your Internet marketing strategy that continually builds trust and confidence by meeting the psychological marketing needs of that visitor and potential customer while escorting that visitor through the selection and purchasing process.

Creating a successful online sales process can be accomplished by making sure that you represent and court your visitor through the five levels of the sales process on your site.

Anyone who has studied any marketing at all knows that there are psychological needs that must be met in order for a person to be persuaded to purchase a product or service.

If it's a product you are selling are you representing that product to solve a specific problem or meet a specific need? If you are selling a service are you getting in touch with the pain of your potential client to draw their interest into what you are offering?

There are steps that you can take to effectively do that and in response witness the successful sales process over and over in the virtual world that is why an Internet marketing strategy is a necessity not an option.

The five levels of the sales process build on one another in many ways. An Internet Marketing Strategy that is done correctly will clearly define all five levels of the process and how they are represented through your site. The strategy will then assist you in setting realistic and attainable Internet marketing goals. It will also assist you in using each step to build and influence the others so that the process continually moves toward the successful close of the sale.

These five levels of the sales process are the core components that will move your website viewer from visitor to customer or client. By representing each level that is mentioned below and courting your potential client or customer through those levels you will have the power to move your site from failure to success.

— Marketing/Prospecting to your Target Market and Audience

— Build Credibility and Trust - (Your viewer needs this to move forward)

— Escort and Court the Buyer through the Process - (Meet their Needs 7 out of 10 want to buy!)

— Present the Product or Service that meets their needs

— Successfully Close the Sale

Let's explore each phase in depth, so that you have a greater understanding of how you can put these princples to work for your business.

Level 1: Marketing/Prospecting

Prospecting is the result of your marketing. It's the delivery of targeted qualified traffic to your virtual storefront. This can be achieved by search engine optimization, pay per clicks, or advertisements that draw people to your site. Once they are there it is your job and responsibility to deliver your Unique Selling Proposition. Not sure what your USP is? Ask yourself the following questions:

— What is the obvious void in the marketplace that your product or service fills?

— What makes your business stand out as distinct and appealing that sets your business apart from the rest?

Level 2: Build Credibility and Trust

In a brick and mortar business trust is built by human interaction. Greeting a person when they walk in the door or physically helping them find something that they are looking for, so how can you build that same trust and credibility virtually? Your viewer is unconsciously judging your credibility by mentally asking themselves the following questions:

— Does this feel and look professional like a legitimate company?

— Is this site reliable?

— How fast is it downloading and are there broken images or links?

— Can I find my way through the site with the navigation that is provided, or are these virtual isles cluttered?

— How is the copy on this site?

— Is it powerful, does it draw me in or is obvious that there was no time taken to write it?

— Are there spelling and grammatical errors?

— Do the images draw me in or are they distracting and irrelevant?

— Can I find the companies assurances and privacy policies easily?

— What about customer support? Is it easily found?

— Can I access support and information that I need easily or is it hidden?

Are you guiding your viewers or are you leaving them in the dark. Your site should work as a personal shopper, a live virtual assistant that knows the needs that your visitor has and makes the solutions for those needs easily accessible.

Level 3: Escort and Court the Buyer

A person who visits your site has been targeted if you followed the first steps in prospecting, so now it's time to qualify the visitor. How do you do this? It's actually very easy. A person happens on your site because they are looking for a solution to a problem. That solution can be a product or a service. Internet marketing studies show that 7 out of 10 visitors to a site are ready to buy. Take the time to escort and court them to what they need.

— When you look at your current site are you helping your visitors to identify and find the best solution for that problem?

— Are you guiding them to find what they need to solve the problem that they have?

Your navigation should be structured to help those that know exactly what it is that they are looking for, those who know what they want in general but aren't sure about the specifics, and those that are browsing and need you to give them some direction.

Level 4: Present the Product/Service

The presentation process is how you are presenting your products or services to your visitors as you guide them through the selection process after you have escorted them and found out what their needs are in the previous stage. It's important to remember that each level ofthe process overlaps. As you present your products or services to your visitor, be sure that you are continually keeping their attention and interest by motivating them to continue with the sale.

Level 5: Close the Sale

Does your site close the sale effectively? Take a look at each product that you offer, are you providing enough information about the product are you giving them assurance policies and/or guarantees regarding their purchase? Are your product descriptions enticing? Does your description answer common questions that visitors might have? Consider adding testimonials for each product or service to build added credibility.

One thing that many e-commerce sites forget to do is provide payment information. Do you take credit cards, if so which ones? Can I pay you by electronic check? What if I want to mail my check to you, can I do that? Take the guess work out of the purchase. Another vital part of the close that is often missed is clearly communicating your guarantee and assurance that you will stand behind the product or service. If you represent each level that is mentioned above and effectively court your potential client or customer through the five levels you will have the power to move your website from failure to success.

Effects of Internet Marketing Strategy

Having a Internet marketing strategy gives you a measurable and definitive way to target your market and position your business so that those looking for what you have to offer are finding you easily. This is only the first level of the sales process, but it is vital to the success of your online business, but remember traffic marketing is not sales.

Traffic can be increased by search engine optimization, using pay per clicks, or marketing your site in advertising campaigns. After completing the marketing step which brings the traffic you must then turn your attention to selling to your visitor once they get there.

How are you approaching those prospective clients and customers that are visiting your site? Are you persuading them to take the action that you want them to take? Have you defined what it is that you want them to do? Perhaps you want them to...

Buy a product? Request more information? Subscribe to your newsletter or request a free report? There are proven methods and tactics that you can use online to increase your conversion rate and get that prospect to become a customer or client. If you haven't taken time to plan your Internet Marketing Strategy you have made a costly mistake that could be draining to your business and costing you customers. Consider this "What is the annual worth of one customer to you?" Is it $25, $250, or perhaps $2500? If having an Internet Marketing Strategy would help you cultivate and convert just 1 new customer each week would planning that strategy be worth it to you?

Truth is that Internet Marketing differs in many degrees from traditional brick and mortar marketing, but there are a few strategies that remain the same and must be present in order for your online marketing to be successful. For example consider the following:

When marketing virtually you are missing a key component to the sales process. Do you know what one thing is lacking and could cause a potential problem and cost you a loss of sales if not approached with a real solution? The answer is human interaction. This has been the biggest struggle to e-commerce businesses online. Let's think about this for a moment. When a person enters a physical store they are met with the interaction of a sales person. Face-to-face contact takes place and over 90% of normal communication between the two people is non-verbal.

Importance of Internet Marketing

Would you start a business without a business plan? Would you place your yellow pages ad in an irrelevant category just to see if anyone would call? Would you pay thousands of dollars to have a billboard ad created and placed where there is no traffic? If you are among the majority of business owners you probably answered no to all of the above questions. Businesses are very careful when it comes to spending marketing dollars, but truth is most businesses have neglected the most effective marketing tool that they have which is the strategic planning of their internet presence. It's not a problem to spend thousands of dollars to pay for the design and development but the planning process and strategy building has been neglected. Why? Many are under the misconception that a web designer is an expert in the area of Internet marketing and that they are also well versed in search engine optimization.

They are only met with disappointment. Do you know anyone who has experienced following problems:

— Minimal sales and conversion.

— Traffic to the site is not as expected or hundreds of dollars are being paid for traffic leads but still there is no conversion from that traffic.

— Subscriptions to reports or newsletters that you offer are slim to none.

— You've received only minimal requests for services or products by email or telephone since your site launch.

5

Marketing without Advertising

Marketing means running a first-rate business and letting people know about it. Every action your company takes sends a marketing message. A clever ad is what pops into most people's minds when they think about getting the word out about their business.

There are about 20 million nonfarm businesses in the United States. Of these, about two million are involved in construction; another five million deal in wholesaling, manufacturing, trucking, or mining. A small minority (30% of the total) generate customers by advertising. The rest rely on personally knowing their customers, on their reputations, and sometimes on salespeople or commissioned representatives.

Of the remaining 13 million businesses, 70% are run by one person. It's very rare for the self-employed to find advertising useful; the single-person business, whether that of a lawyer, doctor, or computer consultant, relies almost exclusively on personal recommendations. That leaves the percentage of businesses who might even consider advertising useful at less than 19%. We think most of them don't need it, either.

There are four main reasons why advertising is inappropriate for most businesses:

— Advertising is simply not cost-effective. Claims that it produces even marginal financial returns are usually fallacious.

— Customers lured by ads tend to be disloyal. In other words, advertising does not provide a solid customer base for future business.

— Dependence on advertising makes a business more vulnerable to changes in volatile consumer taste and thus more likely to fail.

— Because a significant percentage of advertising is deceptive, advertisers are increasingly seen by the public (both consciously and unconsciously) as dishonest and manipulative. Businesses that advertise heavily are often suspected of offering poor quality goods and services.

Advertising's Effectiveness

The argument made by the proponents of advertising is almost pathetically simple-minded: If you can measure the benefits of advertising on your business, advertising works; if you can't measure the beneficial effects, then your measurements aren't good enough. Or you need more ads. Or you need a different type of ad. It's much the same type of rationalization put forth by the proponents of making yourself rich by visualizing yourself as being prosperous..If you get rich immediately, you owe it all to the system (and presumably should give your visualization guru at least a 10% commission). If you're still poor after six months, something is wrong with your picture. It reminds us of the man in Chicago who had marble statues of lions in front of his house to keep away elephants: "It works," he said. "Ain't no elephants in this neighbourhood."

James B. Twitchell, the author of *Adcult*, notes, "Although elaborate proofs of advertising's impotence are available, the simple fact is that you cannot put a meter on the relationship between increased advertising and increased sales. If you could, agencies would charge clients by how much they have increased sales, not by how much media space they have purchased."

Paradoxically, even though some small business owners are beginning to realize that advertising doesn't work, many still advertise. Why? For a number of reasons: because they have been conditioned to believe that advertising works, because there are no other models to follow, and because bankers expect to see "advertising costs" as part of a business proposal.

It's important to realize that your judgment regarding advertising is likely to be severely skewed. You have been surrounded by ads all your life, and you've heard countless times that advertising works. To look at advertising objectively may require you to re-examine some deeply held beliefs.

According to *E* magazine, advertising budgets have doubled every decade since 1976 and grown by 50% in the last ten years. "Companies now spend about $162 billion each year to bombard us with print and broadcast ads; that works out to about $623 for every man, woman and child in the United States". Information Resources, a global marketing resource firm (www.infores.com), studied the effect of advertising and concluded, "There is no simple correspondence between advertising and higher sales .... The relationship between high copy scores and increased sales is tenuous at best."

To illustrate how pervasive the "advertising works" belief system is, consider that if the sales of a particular product fall off dramatically, most people look for all sorts of explanations without ever considering that the fall-off may be a result of counterproductive advertising.

Skeptics may claim that you simply can't sell certain consumer products — beer, for example — without an endless array of mindless TV ads. The California Raisin Advisory Board ran an ad campaign that produced the most recognized ad in the history of advertising. In the mid 1980s, its advertising agency, Foote Cone and Belding, used the first popular national clay animation campaign. The annual budget was over $40 million. The dancing raisins and their song "I Heard It on the Grapevine" created such a popular image that sales from dolls, other toys, mugs, and secondary products generated nearly $200 million in revenue and resulted in a Saturday children's television program using the raisin characters. Raisin sales went up for the first two years of the campaign, largely because cold breakfast cereal marketers were so impressed with the popularity of the ad campaign that they increased the raisin content of their raisin cereals and joined in the advertising.

The Internet and World Wide Web have introduced a new test of advertising effectiveness. Billions of dollars had been spent on advertising before the advent of the Web, yet no major offline advertiser was able to create an online presence of any significance. Even Toys "R" Us, the major American toy retailer, ranked far behind eToys in brand awareness online, despite the fact that Toys "R" Us is a 25-year-old company and eToys lasted barely two years. For Toys "R" Us, decades of advertising simply had no staying power. One of the biggest successes on the Internet, eBay, used no advertising at all.

The hugely successful Craigslist is a community-based operation headquartered in San Francisco. Eminently useful, the on-line bulletin board accepts classified ads for just about anything, from jobs to apartments, football tickets to electronics. What is noteworthy about Craigslist is that it lets users post the vast majority of these classifieds for free — only job ads posted in three United States cities require a fee. It also has an unadorned, simple website and does no advertising.

Craig Newmark started his list ten years ago as a way to keep friends aware of events in the Bay Area. Craigslist now has websites in 65 cities in the United States, and prompted by users' feedback, also has sites in Toronto, Paris, Belgium, Tokyo, and Sydney, with more planned in the near future. One magazine with a significant audience on the Internet is *Consumer Reports*, a magazine that carries no advertising. By eliminating advertising from its business model, *Consumer Reports* is able to maintain a high degree of integrity and cultivate trust among its readers, who value the magazine's objective information.

One giant aircraft manufacturing company, to look at the effectiveness of heavily advertising an in-house computer service through one of its subsidiaries, conducted a survey to find out how its 100 newest customers had found out about it. The results: 13% of these new customers came because of the advertising campaign, 23% because of sales calls, 56% signed up because of recommendations from other satisfied customers and professionals in the field, and 8% weren't sure why they had chosen that computer service.

This is actually a fairly common survey result. Yet, as we can see from their bloated advertising budgets, very few companies act on the information. If they did, they would obviously budget funds for promoting personal recommendations. Indeed, some businesses are apparently so unwilling to believe what market research tells them — that personal recommendations work and advertising doesn't — that they spend money on ads like the one on the following page.

Google is one of the most successful companies in history. Started by two students on credit card borrowings, and bootstrapping the business at every point along the way, the company became profitable in its third year. It was worth $50 billion in a little over five years, with fewer than 2,000 employees. As part of its no-advertising commitment, Google has kept its opening search page refreshingly stark, white, and blatantly free of ads. It also doesn't accept advertising (like banners on Yahoo). It only sells *listings,* and the listings are kept separate from the search results and have no influence on them. This policy is virtually unheard of in magazines, TV, and newspapers.

It's not only large national corporations that are disappointed in the results of advertising. Local retail stores that run redeemable discount coupons to measure the effectiveness of their advertising usually find that the business generated isn't even enough to offset the cost of the ad. Despite this, supporters of advertising continue to convince small business owners that:

— The ad could be improved; keep trying (forever).

— All the people who saw the ad but didn't clip the coupon were reminded of your business and may use it in the future. Keep advertising (forever).

— The effects of advertising are cumulative. Definitely keep advertising (forever).

But what about the favorable long-term effects of continuous advertising? Isn't there something to the notion of continually reminding the public you exist? Dr. Julian

L. Simon, of the University of Illinois, says no: "[attributing] threshold effects and increasing returns to repetition of ads constitutes a monstrous myth, I believe, but a myth so well-entrenched that it is almost impossible to shake."

Using advertising to make your business a household word can often backfire; a business with a well-advertised name is extremely vulnerable to bad publicity.

Take the Coors brewery as an example. Thirty years ago, after it had vastly expanded its original territory and become a household word throughout much of the country with heavy advertising ($100 million per year in the 1980s), the Teamsters' Union waged a very effective consumer boycott against it. In Seattle, a strong union town, less than 5% of the market in the 1990s was drinking Coors. The Coors of the 1960s, known primarily to its loyal customers in the Rocky Mountain states, where it had a third of the beer-drinking market, was far less vulnerable to such a boycott.

Or how about the stockbroker E.F. Hutton, which spent many millions creating a false advertising image: "When E.F. Hutton talks, people listen." The image backfired spectacularly when Hutton was caught engaging in large-scale illegal currency transactions. The many jokes about who really listens when E.F. Hutton talks contributed to the dramatic decline of the firm, which was ultimately taken over by another broker at fire sale prices. Similarly, the huge but little-known agricultural processing company Archer Daniels Midland, headquartered in rural Illinois, made itself a household name by underwriting public television programs. The public was well acquainted with "ADM, Supermarket to the World," by the time it became embroiled in a price-fixing scandal and had to pay $100 million in fines.

Becoming a brand name has its disadvantages. Martha Stewart, the self-promoted diva of gracious living, saw herself ridiculed, and her business empire plunge in value, after she was accused of improper stock trading. The moral of these little stories is simple: If these companies had relied less on advertising, their problems would have been much less of a public spectacle.

Sadly, many small businesses make sacrifices to pay for expensive ads, never being certain they are effective. Sometimes this means the quality of the business's product or service is cut. Other times, business owners or employees sacrifice their own needs to pay for advertising. We think it's far better to use the money to sponsor a neighbourhood picnic or take the family on a short vacation or to put the money into a useful capital improvement to the business. As John Wanamaker, turn-of-the-century merchant and philanthropist, put it, "Half the money I spend on advertising is wasted, and the trouble is, I don't know which half."

Traditonal and Modern Aspects of Advertising

Perhaps the worst aspect of traditional advertising, one apparent to anyone who runs a retail store, is that customers who respond primarily to media ads don't usually return. The same truth has been discovered by magazines and publishing companies that rely heavily on junk mail solicitations to sell their wares. The fact is that customers recruited through scatter-gun advertising techniques such as TV spots, newspaper ads, direct mail, contests, unsolicited telephone sales, and Internet freebies rarely come back. Unscrupulous Internet businesses such as DoubleClick have used the Internet to invade your privacy and sell your email address to other businesses who besiege you with so-called "targeted" marketing based on sites you have visited and purchases you have made.

An example of this phenomenon familiar to most owners of small service-type businesses comes from the experience of Laura Peck. She wrote to us that she used to advertise her assertiveness workshops, but due to financial problems discontinued the ads. Instead, she started cultivating her own community of friends and acquaintances for clients. Two years later, her business was thriving, and she noted:

> "When I advertised, I seemed to attract people who came because of the discount I offered. These clients often did not return, would cancel sessions and generally were not repeaters. The people who were most enthusiastic, most loyal and continued with their sessions were almost always clients who had been personally referred. Had it not been for the economics involved, I would probably not have learned this important lesson: Personal recommendation is the best advertising there is."

To an extent, advertising is an addiction: Once you're hooked, it's very difficult to stop. You become accustomed to putting a fixed advertising cost into your budget, and you are afraid to stop because of a baseless fear that, if you do, your flow of new customers will dry up and your previous investments in advertising will have been wasted.

While of course there are rare occasions when a particular ad can produce lots of business, it's as rare in the small business world as catching a 30-pound lake trout off a recreational fishing boat or winning a $100,000 jackpot at a gambling casino. The story of the great advertising success (the "pet rock" fad of years ago is an extreme example) becomes widely known in the particular community and is picked up by trade journals and sometimes even the general media. As a result, many inexperienced business people are coaxed into spending money on ads.

Overlooked in all the hoopla is the rarity of this sort of success; also overlooked is what often happens to the person whose ad produced the quick profits. Flash-in-the-pan advertising success may bring an initial influx of customers that your business isn't prepared for. This usually has two unfortunate consequences: Many loyal long-term customers are turned off when service declines as the expanding business stretches itself too thin, and most of the new customers will not be repeaters.

Mary Palmer, a photographer in San Jose, California, started her business with a simplistic but traditional marketing strategy — advertising on her local newspaper's "weddings" page. Palmer was one of the first photographers in her area to insert an ad for wedding photos. She very happily took in $12,000 during the prime April-to-August wedding season. The next year she advertised again, but this time her ad was one of many. Not only did the ad fail to generate much business, she got few referrals from the many customers she had worked for the previous year.

Palmer's business is in direct contrast to Gail Woodridge's, who also specializes in wedding photography. Woodridge doesn't do any advertising in the conventional sense, although she does list her services widely in places likely to produce referrals. Her clients are primarily referred to her by wedding planners, bridal gown and flower stores, friends, and former clients — people who know her and trust her to do a good job. Since this approach has meant that her business has grown fairly slowly, she has had the time, and the good sense, to make sure that the many details of her business are in order, including her office work and finances, as well as her camera equipment, darkroom supplies, and filing system.

According to a recent consumer expenditure survey, households spend $4 trillion per year. It's estimated that $236 billion will be spent this year in the United States on print, radio, online, and broadcast advertising to get a piece of this market. The result is sensory bombardment. It is also estimated that each American is exposed to well over 2,500 advertising messages per day, and that children see over 50,000 TV commercials a year. In this view, as many as one-quarter of all these ads are deliberately deceptive. Increasingly, the family of businesses that advertise is not one you should be proud to be associated with.

According to Joan Price, in her book *The Honest Truth About Losing Weight and Keeping It Off*, 90% of dieters regain their lost weight within one year. She explains, "Sorry, folks, there's no miracle way to block, burn, rub, jiggle, vacuum, melt or wrap fat off our bodies. There's no magic pill, injection, cream or potion. If there were, don't you think it would make the front page of all the newspapers and medical journals instead of being buried in an ad?" Nowhere in the ad is there a mention of permanent weight loss, because, of course, whatever the method it won't work over the long term. If the ad told the truth, no one would use the service.

An ad that duped our friends, who bought their son a highly advertised remote control car for Christmas. It had just hit the market, and our friends joined the long line at the checkout stand picturing the delight on their child's face Christmas morning. It was not clear to our friends from the ads that the car needed a special rechargeable battery unit, and when they returned to the store a week before the big day they were informed that the batteries were sold out and wouldn't be available until after Christmas. They went back week after week until finally, two months after Christmas, the batteries arrived. To add insult to injury, the charger unit for the $50 car cost an extra $20.

An ad that offers home security at a bargain price in big letters sounds like just the ticket to protect your family, until you read the fine print. In very tiny letters, the ad explains that the $99 price covers only the standard installation and that an additional 36-month monitoring agreement is also required. In addition, a telephone connection fee may also be required. Obviously, whether you look in a newspaper, a magazine, or the electronic media, it is not difficult to find many less-than-honest ads. Even if you advertise in a scrupulously honest way, your ads keep bad company.

The public, which has long since become cynical about the general level of honesty in advertising, will not take what you say at face value. For example, suppose you own a restaurant, and instead of extolling the wonders of your menu in exaggerated prose you simply state that you serve "excellent food at a reasonable price." Many people, cynical after a lifetime of being duped by puffed-up claims, are likely to conclude that your food couldn't be too good if that's all you can say about it.

But some warn against combating the cynicism with trickery. For example, in a *Time* magazine article titled "It's an Ad Ad Ad World" (July 23, 2002), Keith Reinhard, chairman of marketing services agency DDB Worldwide, stated, "I'm against any form of deception. In the end, it's bad business." One type of dishonest advertising is especially irritating because it's a bit more subtle and involves magazines and newspapers that you might have respected before you discovered their policy. It works like this: The publication touts the products and services of its advertisers in its news stories. For example, some computer magazines have been known to favorably review the products of their heavy advertisers, and small newspapers often fawn over the products and services of businesses that can be counted on to buy space. Once you discover this sort of policy, everything the publication reviews, even businesses that are truly excellent, is thrown into question.

Devious advertising is rampant in our culture; from "enhanced underwriting" of public broadcast shows, featuring announcements that look identical to commercial television ads, to paid product placement (inserting brand-name goods into movies and TV).

Stealth or covert marketing in which hypes and allegiances are hidden from view is the latest fad. For example, stealth positions celebrities on talk shows praising prescription drugs without mentioning that a pharmaceutical company is paying them. No longer satisfied with product placement on TV and in movies, companies now pay authors to include brand names in the text of their books. And it gets worse as the line between life and advertising blurs. Trendsetters are paid to drive cars to important parties. Attractive people are hired to frequent bars and talk up certain brands. Moms are paid to praise products at soccer games, and teens are hired to give their peers tee shirts, posters, and CD samplers hyping bands.

Indeed, we have come a long way from the dairy industry giving free milk to children at recess. School districts across the country now sell exclusive ad space to the highest bidder on school buses, hallways, vending machines, and athletic uniforms. Channel One, which gives participating schools video equipment in exchange for piping ads into the classroom, is the tip of the iceberg. Corporations have begun writing the very lesson plans themselves.

Thirty years ago, a study done for the Harvard Business School made clear how the American public felt about traditional advertising: "43% of Americans think that most advertising insults the intelligence of the average consumer. And 53% of Americans disagree that most advertisements present a true picture of the product advertised." The chief reasons for hostility to advertising are that it is intrusive and patronizing (73%), morally objectionable (50%) and false and misleading (36%). That the judgment of the general public about honesty in advertising has not improved is demonstrated by a 2004 Gallup study asking: which professionals does the public trust the most, and the least. Advertising professionals were second to last, and used car salespeople came in last.

If you want to know who is really behind an ad campaign that appears to be advocating better public policy or medical care, refer to Annenberg Public Policy Center's website at: www.appcpenn.org. Let's take a minute to look at the advertising slogans of some of America's most prominent corporations. People are apparently so sick of traditional advertising hype that occasionally even counter-advertising is successful. Bernie Hannaford, who runs a diner named "The Worst Food in Oregon," was quoted in *USA Today* as saying, "I'm a lousy cook, and my father always told me to tell the truth, no matter what." Signs outside invite diners to "Come in and sit with the flies!" and warn, "Food is terrible — service is worse."

Honest Ads

Lest you become completely discouraged about the possibility of a better standard of honesty in advertising, there is hope. At least two nations, Japan and Sweden, encourage honesty in their advertising. In neither country do ads have "fine print" that contradicts the main message, nor do they permit the sorts of puffery and hype we are used to and which all too often amount to little more than lying.

Japan's tradition of honest advertising is a long one. In the first century A.D., Chinese visitors were so impressed with the honesty of Japanese businesses that they recorded it as a main attribute of their culture. This 2,000-year-old history of honesty is today reflected in many details: Restaurants display samples of their food in the window and quote prices in round numbers, including sales tax and tip. If you see an 800-yen price advertised for an item, it is the total price you pay. Nolo's Stephanie Harolde, who lived and worked in Japan, adds that Japanese businesses never put down their competitors or used comparisons that intimated their product was better than the competitors'.

In Sweden, whose culture is closer to our own, there has been a more deliberate political decision to foster truthful advertising. In that country, it has been against the law since the early 1970s to be deceptive in advertising. To accomplish this, the government not only extended its criminal code to proscribe deceptive advertising, but also formed an administrative agency to enforce the law. As a result, the Swedish people now strongly defend the integrity of their advertising. Perhaps someday we, too, will be proud of ours.

Deceptive advertising is technically illegal in the United States, but enforcement is minimal. The legal standards for advertising are discussed in *Legal Guide for Starting & Running a Small Business*, by Fred Steingold (Nolo). The Japanese and Swedish use of advertising to urge that, should you ever decide to advertise, be sure your advertisements are scrupulously honest and as distinct as possible in style, content, and location from the general run of other ads. For example, if you limit an offering in a print ad in any way, do so in print as large as the offer itself. If you advertise a service, don't overstate the likely beneficial result of using it, and include a warning as to any risk.

Branding

"Branding" has been a catch phrase in advertising for the past decade, and brand managers can now be found in the marketing departments of large companies. Branding is an ingenious response to the fact that traditional advertising doesn't work. The idea is to make a product or service so well known that its consumer recognition magically places it in the category of widely recognized and respected brands. The concept of branding is that a minor brand, Electronic Product X, can become as well known as a major brand such as Sony Electronics if Electronic Product X simply spends enough in advertising to "establish" its brand name.

The problem with this concept is that true brand identity is created when a company produces quality products or services and stands by them with solid warranties, product recalls, and other methods to ensure customer satisfaction. Running a business this way — not spending a fortune on advertising — is what creates trust and goodwill. In recent decades, several brand names were devastated when they did a lousy job of handling problems with their products. Perrier, Gerber baby products, Sears Auto Centers, and Firestone each mismanaged product recalls and took years to recover. Gerber was ultimately sold to new management, and Sears even damaged the reputation of its nonauto business. On the other hand, Tylenol handled a recall beautifully and made its brand even stronger.

For a branding strategy to be effective, a company must be vigilant about its product and service quality — and be prepared for emergencies. Without addressing these issues, a company's reputation is a sitting target, waiting to be ruined. No amount of advertising will be able to develop a good reputation for a company unless there's solid product integrity behind it.

In an article on branding in *The New Yorker,* James Surowiecki stated, "Where modern marketers have succeeded, wildly, is in selling us on the idea that marketing is all you need. The numbers suggest a different, homier lesson. The surest way to get stronger sales is to sell a stronger product."

"Hey, wait a minute," you may be saying. "Traditional media advertising may not be as worthwhile as it's cracked up to be, but many types of advertising do work for small businesses."

The types of "ads" that often work for small businesses include the telephone Yellow Pages, business directory listings, flyers posted in laundromats, good Internet Web pages, and "notification" type ads placed in all sorts of appropriate locations, from free "penny saver" newspapers to, in the case of a restaurant with late evening hours, the program of the local symphony.

There is a major distinction between these types of ads directed at interested prospects and traditional print, broadcast, and electronic advertising. In fact, we prefer to call these sorts of notices, whether paid for or not, "listings." One good rule to distinguish the two is that a listing is found where people are looking for it. A traditional ad, on the other hand, like a billboard in front of some lovely scenery or a deodorant commercial in the middle of an engrossing TV show, is usually intrusive and often annoying.

Another aspect of traditional advertising, but not of listings, is that advertising agencies get what amounts to a kickback for selling an advertisement: They make most of their money from the discount the media offers only to them. For example, an ad agency might sell you an ad for $100,000 and then buy media time for $85,000. If you list your business in the Yellow Pages, even using a large ad, you and the ad agency are charged the same rate. Putting up a successful website can draw hundreds of thousands of viewers, even if you create it yourself. In other words, listings almost never have an ad agency discount policy.

To further illustrate the distinction between advertising and listing, consider the popularity of TiVo and TiVo-like products. TiVo lets the user skip the advertisements — a feature most users take advantage of. Advertising is an intrusion on nearly everyone's time, and most people don't like the intrusion no matter how cute, funny, or interesting the ad is. A listing, on the other hand, is always in a place that a prospective customer goes to for the purpose of finding information, like the Yellow Pages. A Google placement is the ultimate listing, because the prospective customer is looking for the specific word or words that define the information search.

Alex Gault, wrote an article about the effectiveness of Google's AdWords program for marketing purposes:

"Throughout the twentieth century most ad campaigns depended upon the following practices: demographic analyses by marketers, media selection by media planners, ad placement by media buyers, and then analysis of results by agency executives. All told, a campaign and its assessment took many months.

"With the Google AdWords program, an analogous process can take mere days. A shoe marketer like Nike might select 3,000 keywords — "pronation," "distance running," "Michael Jordan," etc. — and write five messages for each keyword. It's thus not unheard of to have 15,000 pieces of creative for just one product. The messages for each keyword alternate, and the ones that result in the least hits are eliminated. Feedback can be almost instantaneous. 'Overnight you can see which ads work best and shut some off,' says Tim Armstrong, VP of ad sales at Google. 'And there's no penalty for trying every idea, because you only pay for what works.' Unless they run out of a product, advertisers have no incentive ever to shut off a campaign."

Indeed, for most businesses, listings are essential, particularly Yellow Pages ads for businesses that people use primarily in an emergency: a drain cleaning service, a plumber, or a locksmith, for example. Listings in the phone book Yellow Pages — and, where appropriate, the Silver Pages for seniors and ethnic Yellow Pages — are invaluable.

Also, if you have an online business, be sure to list it in directory sites. Online directories are like traditional Yellow Pages in that they are organized by subject — making it easy for anyone to find your construction, editing, or daycare business. To check out the directory that already lists the competition — and to get ideas about how and where to list your own business — do a search using Google (www.google.com) or some other search engine under "Online Yellow Pages Directories."

In a few instances, the concepts of listing and advertising have all but merged. For example, in many areas of the country, Wednesday is traditionally the day grocery stores put items on sale. Thrifty shoppers therefore check the full-page lists (ads) of items for the best bargains. Similarly, in the computer software business, a great deal of software is sold at discount prices by companies that regularly advertise their wares in computer magazines. The ads feature, in very small print, long lists of available software. Sophisticated customers know to check these listings first whenever they need software, because the prices offered are usually lower than in retail stores.

The Chamber of Commerce, employment and rental agencies, professional newsletters, magazines and journals, and special interest books, such as those geared to the writer or photographer, are commonly accepted places to list goods or services. And in some instances, newspapers have developed such strong special-interest sections that it also makes sense to list one's services there. For example, a travel agency specializing in charter flights to Asia might place a list of prices in the Sunday travel section. Similarly, small community newspapers exist primarily thanks to local advertising, which usually consists of listings of goods and services. Many merchants find that this type of listing produces good results. Local schools and theater groups also depend on the support of the business community. We consider those kinds of ads as listings of the best sort.

The Common Ground directory, a very successful cooperative enterprise that publishes information in newspaper form about businesses involved in personal transformation. Interested people subscribe or pick up a copy at coffee shops, health spas, or wherever the businesses listing in Common Ground feel it is appropriate to leave a stack of papers. Since distribution is taken care of by the people who list in the directory, the paper has an uncanny ability to be located exactly where people who are interested in the services listed are likely to find it.

Nonprofits face the same challenge that for-profit businesses do: They need to tell as many people as possible about the service or product they provide. The Palo Alto, California, Information & Referral Service has come up with a clever way to disseminate a lot of information in a convenient package. It puts out an easy-to-use directory that lists some 200 local agencies and organizations and gives the Service's number for further information.

It's important also to realize that listing can take lots of forms other than paid space in publications. For example, in many areas, if your cat or dog runs away from home, you list this fact as poignantly as possible on the corner telephone pole or fence post. This sort of listing is so common that if someone in your neighbourhood finds a pet, she is very likely to check out that same pole or fence. In rural areas all kinds of information is posted in this way. When Salli was out on a walk along her country road recently she noticed a cardboard sign nailed to a pole: "Warning! Don't buy! Carl Chase [not his real name] delivers wet wood and won't return deposit. Ex-buyer." There is nothing new about this. The Romans used to paint information about upcoming gladiator fights on the walls of buildings, and the Greeks posted important notices on rotating columns at busy locations.

For home service businesses such as chimney sweeping, babysitting, and house sitting, the laundromat bulletin board is where many people look for help. Colleges and universities are a good source for language schools, tutors, dance instructors, typists, and roommate referral services. In rural areas, being listed on the Farm Trails Map (a guide for visitors interested in buying agricultural products) is one of the most important marketing tools for people selling fruit, nuts, vegetables, livestock, and Christmas trees. And artists who live in a certain area will print a map along with a short description of their work and host "open studio" weekends. Motels and bed and breakfast inns are good places for many small businesses to be listed as part of the establishment's recommended services.

6

Marketing Plans and Web Site Promotions

Marketing plans can feel like a pain in the neck (not to mention other body parts). Reality is quite the opposite. Small business owners, and others without a boss to impose a due date, often find themselves "too busy" to complete a marketing plan or update the existing one. If this sounds like you, then you are leaving profits on the table and the best thing you can do for your business is finish a 2007 marketing plan. Here are five tips to help you follow through with planning:

Planning Approach

Before you begin, research different options and tools for writing your marketing plan. There are several correct ways to complete a plan. Options range from a simple one-day plan to software-developed plans to detailed company-dictated procedures resulting in a book-length document. Once you have chosen your approach, stick to it. If you begin pulling procedures from several different methods, you may become overwhelmed and never finish. The critical part is completing the plan so you have a strategic document to act from.

Timing

If you do not set aside dedicated time for completing your marketing plan, it will always be pushed to the back burner and never completed. Schedule marketing plan development as you would a meeting. Block time out on your calendar and keep that appointment.

Implementation Measures

Your marketing plan isn't worth the paper it's printed on (or the drive it's stored on) without strong implementation. Following timelines leading up to and evaluating performance during execution can make for smoother implementation.

You can use specialized project management tools to automate timeline creation or do it manually in a spreadsheet or text document. If you are completing a timeline manually, start with the due date and work backwards. Note each major project milestone leading up to completion and the time needed for each component. This will give you intermediate deadlines, so you will know if you fall behind schedule. Leave room for comments and notations about who is responsible for each aspect of implementation.

Also, know how you will measure success, and set up ways to monitor project results. Problems are easiest to solve early on, before the entire budget has been spent and there is time to adjust for improvement.

The place for your marketing plan is "front and center," not in a drawer next to the tax returns. Refer to it often throughout the year as you execute the marketing programs you've planned. This keeps you focused on programs in the plan.

Marketing Opportunities

New marketing opportunities present themselves often. Without a visible plan, you may find yourself darting after opportunities instead of following a strategic plan. Whenever a new opportunity arises, refer to your marketing plan and ask yourself if it fits with one of your marketing strategies. If so, decide (1) which program in your plan it will replace and (2) if funds are best spent on the original or new project. Take these tips to heart and you'll find your business running more smoothly and profitably.

WEBSITE MARKETING PLAN

As opportunities arise or your business environment changes, the objective and marketing strategies in your plan will point you toward the best action. Without a strategic plan, you risk becoming unfocused in your marketing efforts, resulting in guesses about what might be best for your business.

To be most effective, your Website (as well as other) marketing strategies should be a part of your overall business marketing plan. By aligning online marketing with your offline efforts, you can better achieve overall company objectives. Additionally, you will present a consistent style and message across all points of contact with your target audience.

Your strategic focus will in part be determined by your site's status. If you already have a site in place, your plan can focus strictly on marketing issues. In other words, how to most effectively market using your existing site.

If you have a site that needs improvement, however, your marketing efforts will be more effective if you incorporate Website enhancements in with your strategies.

Finally, if you do not yet have a site, you can create one as you develop a marketing strategy, with your plan focused on launching the site. In any case, remember that your objective, strategies, and tactics will change over time as your situation and focus change.

A strategic Website marketing plan is similar to a strategic business marketing plan, but with a narrower focus (i.e. the Website plan focuses on Internet marketing strategy and programs while the overall marketing plan encompasses the entire business).

As with any marketing plan, the online plan includes developing strategies and tactics (also called action plans) that, when implemented, will help you reach your marketing goals. An objective, strategy, and tactic are each progressively narrower in scope:

The *objective* addresses the "big picture". In general terms, your objective answers the question "How will I overcome my main marketing challenge(s)?" If your company's main site-related challenge is figuring out how to use your Website to help build client business, for example, an objective for your online marketing plan could be "To enhance online client service as well as build site awareness and interest with clients."

A *marketing strategy* supports your objective. The strategy defines general approaches you will take to meet your objective. For example, strategies to support the above objective could include 1) improve online communication, information, and education, 2) build awareness of and interest in your company on the Internet, and 3) communicate the Website's existence and advantages to existing clients.

A *marketing tactic* is where the action takes place. Also called marketing programs or action plans, they are the things you will do to bring each marketing strategy to life. Tactics for strategy 2 in the above example (improve online communication, information, and education) could include 1) sharing experience and observations in your industry through participation in discussion boards, 2) offering an email newsletter, and 3) listing/submitting your site to targeted search engines and directories.

By implementing marketing programs that are consistent with your site objective(s) and marketing strategies you improve your chance of business success.

Writing a Market Plan

Do you have a marketing plan for your Website? If not, it is time to think about developing one. A marketing plan helps you make the right day-to-day and long term decisions. Without a marketing plan, it is more likely your Website will be a drain on finances rather than a business builder.

Creating a marketing plan need not be scary or difficult. It does not require a marketing degree or a lot of experience. You do, however, need to put some quality time into your plan. There are different ways to write a marketing plan, one of which is to develop a marketing plan outline using a five step process.

Those five steps are:

— Gather and Analyze Information

— Verbalize Your Main Challenge(s)

— Develop Your Website Objective(s)

— Create Strategies

— Choose Marketing Programs

As you develop your marketing plan outline, fill in the knowledge you gain throughout the five steps.

Step 1: Gather and analyze information.

You will need information about your company, competitors, customers, and other industry players. This includes all you can find about how the Internet is currently being integrated in your industry with respect to products, promotions, pricing structures, and distribution channels. From this information, you can complete industry and SWOT analyses as well as identify your target customers.

Step 2: Verbalize your main challenge(s).

Write down the main Internet related challenges you want to overcome. Referring to these main challenges will help keep you focused while filling your marketing plan outline. You may even want to write your challenges down in question form - "How do we ____________?". When your marketing plan is completed, it will answer the question "How do I address these challenges?"

Step 3: Develop your Website objective(s).

The objective addresses the "big picture". Your objective answers the question "How will I overcome my main marketing challenge(s)?" in broad, general terms. If your company's main site-related challenge is figuring out how to use your Website to help build client business, for example, an objective for your Website marketing plan could be "To enhance online client service as well as build site awareness and interest with clients."

Step 4: Create strategies

Strategies support your objective, defining the general approaches you will take to meet your objective. For example, strategies to support the objective outlined in Step 3 could include 1) improve online communication, information, and education, 2) build awareness of and interest in your company on the Internet, and 3) communicate the Website's existence and advantages to existing clients.

Step 5: Choose marketing programs (tactics).

The programs are where the action takes place - these are the things you will do to bring your strategies to life. Marketing programs to support strategy 2 in the above example (improve online communication, information, and education) could include 1) sharing experience and observations in your industry through participation in discussion boards, 2) offering an email newsletter, and 3) listing/submitting your site to targeted search engines and directories.

The Write Up

Once you have a marketing plan outline developed, if needed, there are numerous ways to do an expanded write up. If you are a company employee, there may be existing format and content you must follow. You can find some write up suggestions in "What to Include in Your Marketing Plan Write Up". After the initial plan is developed, you should treat it as a work in progress. Tweak and adjust as needed in response to changing conditions. Many companies update marketing and business plans annually when developing budgets for the coming year.

Whether you are a one-person shop or part of a good-sized company, having a Website marketing plan can help your business prosper on the Web.

For those new to marketing plans, the thought of writing a marketing plan from start to finish may feel daunting. It need not. The level of detail you choose to include will depend on your resources and situation. If you have extremely limited manpower or other resources, you may be constrained to a "broad brush," basic marketing plan approach. If your plan must support your claims to others in the company, more back-up detail in your marketing plan may be appropriate.

Include a summary at the beginning. Like any business report, your plan write up should begin with a summary. The traditional executive summary is one option. The table makes everyday use of your plan easier. In one glance you can be reminded of your marketing challenges, objectives, strategies, and tactics as well as budgets and deadlines. Also, as your plan evolves throughout the year, the table makes it easier to modify the plan.

Other features of a basic plan include the following:

— Explain your reasoning. Make some reference to why you chose the specific objective(s) and strategies in your marketing plan. This will make it easier to justify the plan to others (if necessary). It will also help you make smarter, strategic decisions.

— Identify your target customers. By doing so, you will be better able to develop effective advertising messages.

— Write one or more positioning statements. In the statement(s), specify the customer needs you are fulfilling, benefits your products/services offer, and features that deliver those benefits.

— Explain key issues and opportunities when you write a marketing plan. These can best be identified through industry and/or competitive analyses.

— Include preliminary budgets and timelines for your action plans / programs.

WRITE AN ADVANCED MARKETING PLAN

By including detailed analysis and arguments to substantiate your plan, you can write an expanded marketing plan:

— Describe the strengths, weaknesses, opportunities, and threats your business faces (SWOT analysis).

— Explain the business environment. What are your competitors' strategies? What potential substitutes are available?

— Include the trends in your industry and how they affect both online and offline activity. Show growth projections.

— Detail the financial aspects when you write the marketing plan. Include break even analysis for your products or company as well as for the tactics included in your plan. Discuss assumptions made when completing your financial analysis. Show how implementation of your plan will be profitable to your business.

— Include a calendar of events that shows milestones in the coming weeks or months.

You can be as detailed or top-line as needed when you write a marketing plan. In any case remember that your marketing plan is always a work in progress. It may be current, but it is never "done."

Improving Online Marketing Presence

Increasingly, online marketing is a crucial part of any marketing plan. Executing the programs in your plan, however, is just as critical. For many, finding the time is difficult. To make progress, you must set time aside each day (or other regular time period) for marketing online.

To that end, take a moment right now to block out time for online marketing over the next six months, beginning today.

Use that time today and over the next six months to execute Internet- based programs in your plan. No plan yet? No problem. You will, of course, want to finish your marketing plan so you can refine your activities, but you can begin improving your online presence today by doing one or more of the following ideas:

Evaluation of Marketing Plan

Business owners often find it difficult to know whether their marketing tactics are working. This can be especially tricky when you use a combination of marketing activities simultaneously, or if using personal-contact tactics such as networking.

No matter what business you're in, your marketing should be accountable. So here's a few ways to evaluate how well you're doing.

1) *Look at your sales (or fee income).* They should be going up! But be careful about what you measure. Some firms have a longer sales cycle than others. To get an accurate picture you might need to also measure the number of new leads being generated, or the number of appointments, or the number of billable hours achieved. Remember discounts or variances in fees will affect total sales values.

2) *Ask your clients.* Check to find out where they heard of you. Most businesses never ask this question and miss out on gleaning valuable insights into how clients select a service provider.

3) *Does your advertising and/or promotional activity produce direct responses?* It should. If your answer is "I don't

know" then you've got some work to do. In addition to 2) above, there are some things you can do to improve response rates.

— Firstly, make sure you are advertising in the right media. Choose media to suit your selected audience. Be as specific as possible. And avoid rejecting options just because they don't look "exciting", such as trade journals that might have relatively small readership. Importantly, check with your audience to make sure they actually do read the publication.

— Use a strong headline that asks a pertinent question, or gives a solution-oriented statement.

— Include a clear call-to-action. Tell people what they should do. For example: Ring today for your free appointment; Ask for our free information sheet.

— Include multiple methods of contact. Phone, email, and web site are all important. Give prospects a choice of how to contact you.

4) Do your networking activities create new opportunities for you? One of the major principles of effective networking is to "give" rather than "sell". That is, you should look to help others as you spread word about your services. But this softly, softly approach can make it hard to measure effectiveness.

To measure your networking activities make sure you track the source of incoming enquiries. Then see if any of your visible/tangible tactics can be credited with generating the enquiry. If not, then maybe you can safely say it was a referral generated by networking. This is made a lot easier if you're a member of a lead-generating club such as BNI or Leads. You'll get specific feedback each week from these groups.

5) Do your marketing tactics make it easier to sell your services? To do this your marketing activities and/or material should do the following:

   — Attract qualified prospects (who have shown a specific interest in your services).

   — Anticipate and diffuse potential questions/ concerns from prospects.

   — Be easy to use when personally selling to prospects. For example: material should be relevant; images/charts easy to understand; and be presented in a format the prospect will be likely to keep.

   — Focus on your client needs and your points of difference (Unique Selling Proposition).

6) Check your sales conversion rate. The best approach here is to look at your historical records and determine whether your conversion (or closure) rate has improved. "Selling" is an important part of the "marketing" function, so make sure you assess your success at closing the sale, rather than just focus on generating new leads.

7) Does your plan have a positive return on investment (ROI)? Does it bring in enough new/repeat business to justify the expense? Rather than just look at the "marketing budget" as one total, you really need to evaluate the cost effectiveness of each specific marketing activity. Even if you think you're getting a great ROI overall, maybe you can do even better by changing or eliminating unproductive tactics.

Profitable Marketing Mix

You may have heard the term "marketing mix" used in connection with marketing planning.

Your marketing mix means the combination of promotions, products, places (distribution channels), and prices you chose for your business. Including both short term and long term strategies in the marketing mix can make for a more profitable business.

Long term strategies build brand/company awareness and give sales revenue a permanent, gradual boost. Short term strategies create a temporary, immediate revenue boost by giving buyers an incentive to purchase.

By implementing both long and short term strategies, you can attend to immediate sales goals while building your business reputation and goodwill. Some examples of both types of strategies are below.

Creating Long Term Marketing Strategies

Branding. General advertisements and other high profile activities contribute to your company's image. These points of contact with your target customer help mold your image, which in turn can create loyalty from your customers.

Philanthropy. Donating money, services, and/or time can build trust and a positive image for your business. Philanthropy contributes both toward your branding efforts and your company's internal well being.

New Product Pipeline. New products in development represent your future sales. If you get feedback from your customers or potential target market, then design new products (or change existing ones) to meet their needs, you are ensuring a demand for your products in the future.

Short Term Marketing Mix Strategies

Reduced Price Sales. Limited time sales encourage customers to act. You likely have customers intending to buy but have not "gotten around to it". Holding a sale will give them incentive to purchase.

Group Discounts and Offers. Discounts or other offers to a specific group can help exposure your business to new customers, resulting in a sales surge.

Pay-Per-Click Search Engines. Pay per click search engines are another way to become visible to new customers. Use them carefully, however. Do not bid more per click than the profit you expect to make from that click.

Role of Search Engines

High search engine placement can produce both short term and long term results. Short term, you can gain immediate sales. Long term, results come as potential business partners find your site. Do not, however, become obsessed with search engine optimization to the detriment of your other marketing strategies. Search engine marketing should be one part of a more comprehensive plan. Include other marketing strategies in your plan to reach additional customers.

Search engine optimization is to hire an outside expert to work on search engine marketing while you focus internally on other parts of the marketing mix. If you take this route, however, be alert for agencies that use tricks that go against search engine guidelines to increase your rankings. They may get you results in the short term, but could get your site reduced in rankings or banned in the long term. Thoroughly research any SEO firm before hiring them to do work on your Website.

These are not the only short and long term strategies you could incorporate into your marketing mix. Look for different ways you can build long term recognition and health for your business. Effectively incorporate those into the marketing mix with a variety of shorter term, sales boosting techniques and your business will thrive.

Lets Start Your Marketing Plan

When developing or updating a marketing plan, knowing where to start is often a challenge. To better develop effective marketing strategies, begin by gathering information about both your business and the larger business environment (competition, trends, statistics, etc). Internally, the amount of information you gather about your own business will depend on your company size. Information can include business strategies and plans; company marketing plans; pricing; and income statements.

Employee knowledge is also a valuable resource. As you gather information, if you at first turn to internal sources then expand your understanding through external resources you will do fine. External information about the business environment often takes the form of existing research, articles, competitive information, and industry news. While these are often available in both print and digital, the focus here is finding information online.

Online Information Gathering

The numerous news sources and billion or so Web pages available on the Internet make finding information much easier than in pre-Internet days. Before the Internet, gathering information meant trips to the library, purchasing expensive publications and reports, and commissioning your own primary research. Now, it is a matter of knowing where to search.

You can start searching the Internet by looking in each of the general areas below. Organize useful material as you find it. Purchase, bookmark, or file each resource so you can draw upon it during marketing plan development. These external resources, together with your internal company information, will be your initial knowledge base as you develop your Marketing Plan. As you progress along the planning process and the specific information you need become clearer, these initial resources are likely to be jumping-off points for gathering more specific information.

Brainstorming Techniques

Truly unique concept development is a struggle, which explains much of the "copying" that goes on within any given industry. Our new business, product and service ideas often have existing products and services as a base, producing only incrementally different results. The key to "breaking out of the box" is creative use of brainstorming techniques, which allows you to see opportunities in a new light.

Brainstorming is a group creativity technique that was designed to generate a large number of ideas for the solution of a problem." Brainstorming business ideas should be uncensored. No idea is dumb or impossible, and each person's contribution is equally valuable. The mail clerk's ideas are as valued as the President's. In order to step outside of the existing business or industry framework, participants must "erase" their memories and pretend they know nothing about what is (or is not) possible. Consider each idea with equal thoughtfulness, no matter how outlandish. The task at hand when brainstorming truly unique business ideas is to free-associate, generating as many ideas as possible.

There's nothing more boring than a sterile conference room. Yet this is where many new business idea / concept development sessions take place, in a room with four blank walls and no stimuli (far from the best atmosphere for brainstorming new ideas). Brainstorming sessions need "springboards" to get the creative juices flowing.

One brainstorming technique for breaking out and generating innovative business, product, or service ideas is to get all of the external senses involved. Try filling colorful gift bags with small items of different textures, tastes, appearances, ingredients, sounds, and smells. In the brainstorming session, break into small groups of three or four people and give each group a bag. Have each group sort through its bag, imagining how the sensory aspects could be incorporated into a new product or other new idea. After about 20 minutes of digging through the bags, discussing, and writing down ideas, allow each group to present their ideas. You will find yourself with many more great ideas than you can execute.

Another approach to brainstorming business ideas is to study trends. Business and general interest publications; the Internet; and trade journals can be effective brainstorming tools for several reasons:

— The general publications contain articles across several industries ? and society in general ? which is good for brainstorming new ideas that can apply to your own industry.

— Business publications often include a mix of short articles (good for brainstorming ideas based on what others outside your industry are doing) and in-depth reports (good for new product concept development based on trends).

— The Internet reflects trends on a real-time basis. Social bookmarking sites and blog directories, track and report the hottest topics. Wordtracker monitors online searches, reporting the top 100 daily.

— By skimming a variety of business related articles (news articles, features, human interest, and analytical pieces) you broaden your idea base, which results in more new product ideas.

Both of these brainstorming techniques can be used for any activity that requires innovative, new business ideas. In addition to new product development, they can be used to generate ideas for online products and services, new marketing strategies, business taglines, and more. No matter what your brainstorming techniques, remember two rules: 1) no censoring and 2) use your senses and current trends as springboards for new ideas. Do this and your brainstorming sessions are sure to be a success.

Marketing Through Website Design

Internet marketing doesn't just involve advertising. Internet marketing also involves making sure a website is properly set up and designed so search engines can locate that website and sequence it in search engine listings. If an internet business website can't be located online that business will likely fail. Marketing a business website by designing it with specific keywords in mind will help that business website become a marketing success.

If you're an internet business owner who designed your business website using HTML programming, otherwise known as hypertext markup language, you may be aware of the importance of meta tags. Meta tags contain keywords and phrases hidden within the coding of websites that contain them. No one viewing a website can see the meta tags, but search engine spiders and meta tag crawlers can read them. Meta tags help search engine technology appropriately place websites on search engine listings. Without well written and properly placed meta tags, an internet business website may never be found online.

There are free search engine tools and meta tag generators for website designers and internet business owners wanting to save money while marketing their website. Free meta tag generators create meta tag codes based on keywords and phrases entered. The meta tags can then be copied and pasted into the HTML coding of the website.

In order for meta tags to be efficient in helping search engine spiders and meta tag crawlers identify a website in search engine listings, a website must contain keywords and phrases. Enough of these keywords and phrases must be contained within website text in order for the website to be sequenced and found online. This is known as keyword density. Five percent keyword density is a good percentage to try and attain. A higher percentage of keywords contained within website text usually result in text that doesn't read well. Marketing a website should begin with marketing a site that makes sense. Don't forego quality of content in exchange for high keyword density.If the content is too redundant and isn't valuable, potential customers will go elsewhere.

There are free keyword density tools that enable website designers and owners to check the keyword density of their websites. Many keyword density tools work by copying and pasting website text directly into a text box and typing the desired keyword in another box. One click of the mouse and the keyword density will be accurately calculated. This free service allows website owners and designers to add the appropriate percentage of keywords to bring density up to the desired number.

After a business website has been properly equipt with meta tags and keywords,website designers and owners can use one of the many free search engine submission services. Free search engine submission services enable people to easily submit their websites to the major search engines. Most free search engine submission services ask those using their service to place a link back to the search engine submission service. This is a nominal request for using this valuable free service.

Marketing an internet business through proper website design is the first step in marketing an online business. Without proper design including meta tags and keyword dense textual content, a business website may end up at the end of search engine listings - if it is even listed at all. Before proceeding with the usual internet marketing methods and techniques, check the internal design of your business website. Good internet marketing begins with good website design.

7

Outsource Content, Analytics and Optimisation

Outsourcing to India has been growing in waves, starting first with software in the late 80s. The next waves were medical transcription and call centers in the late 90s. From the second half of 2003 we have been seeing higher end professional services being outsourced to India. Included in this wave are strategic Internet marketing services. We will take a quick look at the a) potential advantage b) kind of projects and c) the possible problems associated with outsourcing these services to India.

Generally India is known globally for its technical expertise but there are good marketing companies filled with experienced professionals. The technology ethos of India combined in a marketing company creates a foundation for great Internet Marketing Companies.

In addition the Indian Institutes of Management and other top institutions produce some of finest and most sought-after people on the planet. Therefore outsourcing to an Indian company may mean that your project will be in the hands of as high a qualified person as any in your own country. It is hardly necessary to mention the potential cost savings. India has been providing quality services at huge cost savings for years. This is known.

Projects to Outsource

Internet market services can be more than just optimizing web pages for search engines. These hi-end services can include some of the things listed below. These creative services will expand the reach of companies allowing their products and services to penetrate into the offices and homes of potential buyers around the globe giving any entrepreneur or corporation a big competitive advantage.

— Web content development

— Web branding

— Website Optimization

— Web Analytics

— Tutorial creation

— Pop Flash ads

— Online advertising games

— Marketing research

— Online products to increase web traffic

— eBook creation and distribution

— Linking strategies and deployment

— eNewsletter creation and distribution

— Targeting email marketing

— Marketing media product development

— Publishing solutions

— Creative solutions

Problems of Outsource Marketing

Perhaps the biggest problem of outsourcing marketing to India is the lack of a deep understanding of the local market of the customer. This will need to be done by companies who are very close to the market or who can study the market. However globalization is closing this gap.

Outsource Adobe Illustrator and Hand Drawn Illustrations

Mostly media, ad, elearning, publishing or design companies contact us for illustrations. If they do not have the in-house talent they outsource. Conceptualizing and drawing illustrations for school text books- drawing illustrations for a story board that will be used for a movie or training. - creating children's sketches for elearning courses - converting photos to illustrations - drawing cartoons for an animated movie - enriching existing illustrations with color or shadow - converting illustrations to vector - colorizing illustrations and even colorizing CAD - digitizing hand drawings.

The next step is to complete the form on this website. Someone will contact you via email within a few hours (except on Sunday). Ideally we start with a sample to help us understand the project and so that you can measure our quality. We can press from there.

Outsourcing desktop publishing, which is not a core activity in most organizations, is a wise option. Why not let professionals who have the requisite knowledge, equipment, and expertise handle this process for you? Indian companies today can do everything that is done in the West: magazines, books and newspaper layout, cover design, graphics development, development brochures and presentations to name a few.

Projects come in from companies around the world. For example magazine companies that have a monthly magazine send their ongoing layout to India . Real estate companies that produce commercial property brochures are having them designed and developed in India. Publishers of all kinds outsource DTP to India.

Value Additions

This is another advantage of outsourcing to India . Since Indian companies tend to be larger than their western counterparts, they often can do more and provide integrated turn-key solutions. For example they may have individual departments to provide XML tagging, photo services, content writing, editing and proofing.

Outsourcing Desktop Publishing

Not all companies have the resources or expertise to perform this job in house. Outsourcing desktop publishing, which is not a core activity in most organizations, is a wise option. Indian professionals who have the software, equipment, and expertise can do this work for you. The quality of the work has steadily improved and is now at par with international standards. A good Indian company is flexible and can not only take your requirements into account, allowing for last minute changes, but also advise you and offer innovative and distinct solutions.

There are constant advances in computer and printing technology that change and enhance desktop publishing work. Good Indian Service Providers are abreast with these changes and can offer high quality services. They are familiar with electronic publishing technologies, such as XML. Indian companies understand this line of work thoroughly.

In fact, many Indian companies are becoming more advanced than their western counterparts because the sheer volume and diversity of work being outsourced to India. This is causing some companies to grow larger in size and are thus getting broader in their knowledge and experience. Typically the DTP is done by an Indian designer with more than 2 years of experience after having graduated from college. He or she will be Internet savvy and fluent in English.

The customer and vendor ask and answer questions. A sample is requested. Once the sample is complete and the customer approves of the quality and reliability then a price can be established and the project started. Typically the customer has a template and FTPs the template, written content, photos and images and uploads them so that the vendor can download all that is needed to start. The work is completed and a quality check is done and it is returned to the customer for approval. If corrections are required then these are done and the finished product sent to the customer. The final payment is then made.

Most customers initially want to evaluate the quality of the work and the cost. They can request that a simple page be developed and returned. This is also a good way to discover the costs.

Outsourcing Internet Marketing Services

Outsourcing internet marketing services is not a new trend, yet many people are unaware of its potential. There is a lot of uncertainty and scepticism about outsourcing, what many believe to be, a function that should be kept in house. However, there are certain parts of your internet marketing campaign that can be safely outsourced and this article discusses a few of them.

Which Internet Marketing services can you safely outsource? As you are considering this option, some of the questions that might need to be answered would be:

— Would my outsourcing partner have the skills to do this?

— Can I reap immediate financial benefit from this?

— How do I interact with my outsourcing vendor through the lifecycle of the project?

One way of finding the answers is to look at the nature of the service itself. The following are some of the conditions that can determine if a particular service is easy to outsource.

— It should be possible to conceptualize, define and execute the service with the limitation of interacting only over telephone and email.

— The region where the service is going to be outsourced should be known to possess the skills required to implement the service.

— The service should, by nature, require intense human effort and be difficult to automate.

— The service should require people with specific skills and knowledge to implement it.

— It should be easy to monitor the results of this service.

These are some of the services that can be easily outsourced.

Internet Marketing Strategy and Consulting

This is the first on the list since this could be the most controversial. Companies in India are increasingly depending on the internet to acquire customers over the web. For the majority, opening an office in the US or Europe is not feasible. So they have adapted themselves to become the masters of this medium. A lot of people here are well versed with the web and specifically how to market services and products on the web. You could benefit from this understanding. Another good thing is that an Indian company might be willing to provide consultancy as part of their other marketing services.

Search Engine Marketing (SEM)

The objective of this service is to use search engines to drive traffic to your website. By its very nature, SEM is resource intensive. Most of the directories and search engines don't approve of automatic submissions. They prefer manual submission where a person submits a site for approval. To implement SEM in-house requires someone to read up on the tips and tricks and constantly be at it. But then it's not large enough to hire a full time person. Outsourcing this service to professional Internet marketing firm could get you started immediately with very little investment.

However, on a cautionary note, always insist on knowing the way your outsourcing partner implements this service. The industry is full of individuals and companies who spam the search engines for quick results. You would not want to get your website blacklisted by dealing with these companies.

Link Building

This service is closely associated with SEM. Link building requires someone to continuously write to webmasters and requesting them to link to your website. Doing it the right way can take up a considerable amount of time. Link building starts with figuring out why people should link to your website. It then goes all the way to procuring links from other website. The whole exercise can be very time consuming. This service in our opinion is easy to monitor, easy to measure and easy to outsource.

Web Analytics

Using data to make a decision is one thing, but spending

time to collect that data is a different ball game altogether. Web analytics is a service where your vendor is responsible for collecting and analyzing data and making suggestions to you based on the analysis. It makes sense for you, as a business owner, to spend time looking at data and even reports rather than spending time in collecting this information.

Newsletter Campaign

Newsletters are still known to be effective, in spite of the spam menace. Churning out a newsletter every two weeks or every month requires a few things - a system to collect emails, content, a good design, a tool or service to send emails and a system to monitor the effectiveness of the newsletter. So the kinds of skills you are looking at are writing, design and some technology skills. In our opinion, outsourcing this task can make your newsletter campaign extremely effective.

Promotional Writing

As things stand now, content is the king in website marketing. If you want your website to do well, be prepared to invest in original and persuasive quality content. Outsourcing your content to a professional writer could give you immediate benefits. A writer can use your existing website content, your brochure, memos, telephone conversation, emails, etc to either tweak an existing article or produce an original one

Internet Marketing Services

There are several services out there that you can opt for when outsourcing your Internet marketing requirements. We have picked the easiest of the lot. Please get in touch with us if you are interested in outsourcing your Internet

Marketing requirements or even if you would just like to find out more about it.

Website Content Writing

Everyone knows that a website is essential, but a website alone will not generate business or take care of all your requirements. What is necessary is a superior quality and appropriate content that stands out from the rest. That alone can help you generate more traffic and consequently, more business.

Writing for the web is not just a replication of the writing process followed for print media. Website content development incorporates typical writing talent and skills along with search engine optimization. Search engines have algorithms for ranking your website and if you want to get ranked high, you need high quality content on your website and a strategic understanding of how to write keeping the search engines in mind.

Writing and compiling of content for the web can be quite a daunting task. Yet it is a service that can be effortlessly outsourced, thereby adding significant value to your project. With established website content management providers who are experienced at writing specifically for the web, we can ensure that your website will produce desired results. We can assign a writer, an assistant writer or an editor to work for you on an ongoing basis or on a project basis. The cost usually depends on the amount of research and skill required. We can come up with a quote once we receive project details.

Strengths of India web content writers

— *Research at lower costs* - 50% of most writing projects is research. In fact, we can have one team do the research and another do the writing/editing.

— *People* - Shorter time to develop content because more people can be put on the task.

— *Top-quality documentation at a lower cost* - The academic levels of our writers is very high and they include PhDs, MDs, MBAs etc.

— *Talent* - Benefit from a diverse network of talented writers with different styles, insights and training. Indians are global and add that value to content.

— *Qualifications* - Indian writers are well informed and able to write on many subjects. Indians excel in scientific, medical, technical and cultural writing.

— Ability to write fluently in English and many other international languages.

— *Diversity* - Indian writers can develop a wide and diverse range of content because of their International work experience as web content developers, engineers, software programmers, medical doctors, journalists etc.

Risks and Challenges of Outsourcing

Outsourcing to India can be straightforward and entered into with minor risks. The best way to avoid risk is to limit deliverables and payments to small chunks until trust, quality and reliability are established. A sample project is a common way of testing before entering into an agreement.

As in all outsourcing ventures, it is wise to predetermine a clear process to assure quality. A detailed document spelling out exactly what is required often prevents confusion and misunderstandings later on. A good vendor will have a questionnaire or checklist to help capture exactly what you want. In addition to this, he will outline some terms. For example, a good vendor should assure confidentiality, original content and promise not to reuse content. It boils down to trust and the reputation of the vendor. International agreements are useful for clarity but sometimes impractical to enforce.

Outsourcing website content and development entails that you communicate the information clearly. This would mean describing the target audience and what you aim to achieve with the content. Once this is done, there shouldn't be any anomalies in getting your content developed.

When you outsource your content development to India , you are dealing with expert writers who are well trained in English and its nuances. English is their first language and they communicate in English as comfortably as their American or British counterparts. The result is a large number of qualified people who are ready, willing and able to work for global customers.

We have discovered that some fine-tuning may be necessary to meet the exact requirements of the customer. This can be done in a final edit. This tweaking of content may apply to travel writing or lifestyle writing but will generally not be required for medical, scientific or technical writing and other such similar writing/editing.

Privacy and Security Issues

Most of the data privacy and security fears are unfounded. However, one must be aware and deal with credible, well-established content providers. India may not have laws as stringent as those in the US , but the Indian government and other regulatory associations are working towards ensuring that laws are at par with international legislation. One has to understand that Indian companies have as much to lose as their clients if an untoward incident were to occur. The country is not only moving up the value chain by offering more complex services, but is determined to establish its trustworthiness.

You can maximize content and get the most from it by reusing it and repackaging it for a variety of uses. For example from a formal white paper, several other forms of content can be developed: a casual article, an executive summary and a press release. If you already have the necessary content, you can outsource the tiresome task of organizing and preparing this content for use on the web.

Indian Service Providers can modify existing content or reorganize it to meet your needs. This content can be in the form of existing electronic, paper-based or idea-based content. By understanding your products, services or any other needs, content developers can distribute the information on the appropriate pages of your website. Good research, the best keywords, and content tailored according to your requirements, are some features Indian content developers can offer.

Website content includes photographs, articles, stories, audio, illustrations, animations, icons and more. Using this content to communicate clearly, powerfully and create an impact is a major function of every website. Indian Service Providers can provide the following written content development services:

— Copywriting,

— Technical writing,

— Product descriptions,

— Manuals,

— Online help,

— Tutorials,

— Software and technical book writing,

— Game writing,
— Academic writing,
— White papers,
— Grant writing,
— Business writing,
— Report writing,
— Presentations,
— Medical writing,
— Book summary and Book reviews,
— Fiction writing and Book authoring,
— Biography writing,
— Script writing,
— Speech writing,
— News item writing,
— Journalism,
— News release writing,
— Travel writing,
— Promotion leaflets,
— brochures and more . .

8

Methods in Net Equity

Net equity of households in life insurance reserves and in pension funds consists of reserves held against life insurance and annuity policies by insurance enterprises, whether mutual or incorporated, and by pension funds; these reserves are considered to be assets of the policyholders and not of the institutional units that manage them.

Similarities Between Online and Offline Marketing

The first to point out the shared heritage and the similarities between online and offline marketing. From the start, savvy Internet marketers have looked below, rather than above the line to create more effective online campaigns. That's why even the earliest banner ads, because of the way they were targeted, tracked and monetised, were more like direct mailers than advertising. It's not surprising they're so similar. After all, the Internet provides the opportunity for one-to-one communication, for a streamlined fulfilment path, for testing and re-optimising and measuring the results on the bottom line in the same way that direct marketing does. Likewise, it provides an open and accessible platform for communications that advertising and PR professionals have long recognised. So it makes sense that offline marketing would be the platform from which Internet marketing would develop. They have the same DNA but they've evolved in parallel. They have the same principles and the same processes, but different languages and cultures.

Same DNA

First, if the 'ideal' offline marketing campaign, whether it's advertising, direct mail, or PR, it will have:

— *Visibility* - to be seen by the maximum target audience.

— *Functionality* - the mechanics will work.

— *Loyalty* - it will gather data to build rapport.

— *Economy* - it will make money for you.

Likewise, a fully optimised search engine marketing campaign has:

— *Visibility* - to be easy to find.

— *Functionality* - to be easy to use.

— *Loyalty* - it will collect information to develop relationships.

— *Economy* - it will be deliver return on investment.

Same Lifecycle

The principles of search engine marketing, across all four stages of interaction between a web site and its visitors, which the 'optimization lifecycle' are very similar to the interactions between an offline campaign and its audience.

Optimization Lifecycle: In fact, both disciplines are about generating volume and converting it into value through a fulfilment process.

Same Processes

In fact, at practically every stage in any two offline marketing and search engine marketing campaigns, the principles and processes are the same:

— research to qualify the need.

— profiling to identify the message.

— targeting to segment the audience.

— creativity to test effectiveness.

— tracking to measure response.

— interaction to build relationships.

Research to qualify the need

Every campaign, whether online or offline, starts with research to assess market awareness and demand. Offline, this might mean using surveys, polls and market data to find out what people want. Likewise, for a search engine marketing campaign, the search engines data logs can provide a wealth of information. Every search engine which offers Pay Per Click, including Google, eSpotting, Overture and Mirago, allows free and unlimited access to their search logs. This data tells you how many people asked for a particular product or service in the last month, either in the UK alone or internationally, which, as a result, helps you measure the level of awareness and demand for a particular product, service or concept.

Profiling to identify the message

Next, profiling your audience in order to develop the messaging that they'll best respond to, is a vital part of an offline campaign. A combination of resources might be used, such as customer feedback, user and focus groups, as well as statistics from previous campaigns and the copywriter's experience. Likewise, in a search engine marketing campaign, you can use the search engines' keyword research tools to not only find out what people are looking for but how they're asking for it, in their own words.

This is intelligence of the best kind—direct from the people themselves, in their own time. Having access to this kind of intelligence is like talking to the largest, most honest and most unself-conscious focus group in the world, or like having a peek at your future customers' shopping lists. You can not only find out what people want, but the exact words they're using to ask for it, to help refine and enhance your messaging.

Targeting to segment the audience

In offline marketing, targeting, to deliver the right message to the right person, is a fundamental. If you're selling lawn mowers you make sure you don't send mail to people living in flats. If you're selling baby products, you'd focus your PR or advertising campaign on family friendly magazines, rather than lads' mags. It's just the same in an search engine marketing campaign. You can use keyword research to how many people are asking for something, segment your market into groups of people making the same search and create a tailored, search-term specific approach for each. This is interesting because it turns the concept of demographics on its head. It means you can segment your markets and target your marketing based on what people want rather than who they are.

Research from Overture has shown that people use quite different search terms depending on whether they're browsing, comparing or shopping. Someone who is just starting to look for something will use vague, generic searches. If they're planning a holiday, they'll ask for 'cheap flights'. If they're buying a van, they'll ask for a

'Used Transit'. But the further they move along the browsing, comparing and shopping, the more specific their search terms become. They'll start adding locations, channel preferences, makes and model numbers to narrow down the search. Those same holiday buyers will start asking for 'Cheap flights Malaga October' or 'Used Transit dealer Epsom'. You need to make sure that your site is optimised and marketed to catch and convert people at every stage in this buying cycle.

Creativity to test effectiveness

Just as every offline campaign is a mixture of art and science, so is search engine marketing. In all the best TV, poster or direct marketing campaigns, you'd create a choice of creative approaches and test out the response to them, perhaps using an AB list comparison, before rolling out the full campaign. In a search engine marketing campaign, such as a pay-per-click search engine marketing project, having first used keyword research to define the initial creative messaging you can put together a range of test executions and potential keywords to target, then track them which works best. Once the best-performers are identified, strategy, activity and budget can be focused to give the best return.

Tracking to measure response

No self-respecting offline campaign is complete without a decent level of tracking to analyse the response. You'd track incoming orders, 'gone aways' and call centre activity correlated with a corresponding increase in sales. In a traditional PR campaign, you might count column inches and TV and compare it with the cost of an equivalent advertising campaign to measure its relative effectiveness in budget terms. In a search engine marketing campaign, by the same token, you can put cookies on the site, or analyse the server logs, to not only show which creative approaches are getting the best results in terms of conversions, but how long people spent on the site, what they bought, how much they spent, whether they've been before and which page they left from. In offline marketing terms, it's a bit like knowing whether they opened the envelope or read the ad, how long they spent on it, what they did with it afterwards and what they did next.

Interaction to collect information

In many of the offline marketing disciplines, the more information you can collect about a particular target, the more personalised your future communication with them. That's why quite often, the fulfilment of an direct mail or advertising campaign includes collecting information from respondents, whether it's booking a test drive or claiming a free sample. It's just the same in search engine marketing. The objective of a campaign is to drive traffic to a tailored and interactive landing page or micro-site, optimised with plenty of data capture opportunities, to take visitors to the next stage in the fulfilment process.

Integration Pays Dividends

If, like the vast majority of successful brands, you do both offline and search engine marketing, there are plenty of ways you can integrate the two and achieve both better results and economies of scale. In fact, when you're planning, testing managing and reporting on your offline marketing, your search engine marketing company can help you get better results at every stage.

Planning Overall Marketing Strategy

When you're planning your overall marketing strategy, your search engine marketing company can give you a wealth of real-world inside intelligence that you can use in multiple ways. They can monitor search term trends, so you can spot new opportunities ahead of the rest of the market. They can tell you the relative size of market segments, and show you how other web sites are positioning themselves in those markets, so you can size up the competition and devise an effective strategy to win mind and market share. And, of course, they can tell you what your target audience is asking for on search engines, so you can develop more effective creative executions. Likewise, you can focus your PR strategy on what people want to know about you, rather than what you want to tell them, which completely reverses traditional communications paradigms in new and interesting ways.

Testing an Offline Campaign

When you're testing an offline campaign, you can use search engine marketing as a fast and effective proof of concept to gauge the response before the main roll out. Pay per click, whereby you pay a fee to the search engines for every visitor, is the most exact of the Internet marketing sciences and ideal for this kind of test. What you spend and what you get in return, simply by checking your tracking data. It's very quick as you don't have to wait months for the 'natural' or 'organic' results. Pay up front and your ads or sponsored links can be on the search engines, and bringing you vital intelligence you can use offline, within a couple of days.

To put together an online test, your search engine marketing company could use a combination of providers, creative executions and other variables. By tracking visitor behaviour as part of the test, it would also highlight any usability issues with the site that would need to be fixed in advance of the main roll-out. After all, if you're using your web site as the fulfilment path for an offline campaign, you need to be confident that people are being given a warm welcome and the clickstream, from SERPS to data capture to check-out, is as smooth as possible. The information you get from an online test campaign is a vital source of intelligence to help you find weaknesses in the navigation, a lack or relevant content or problems with the check-out or interaction systems before the main campaign, rather than after.

Managing an Offline Campaign

When you're managing an offline campaign and you're using the web as the fulfilment, your search engine marketing company can not only help you:

— attract the maximum qualified visitors but.

— maximise the conversion rate when they get there.

— enhance and protect your brand.

— make yourself heard.

— and give you CRM intelligence to support your future online and offline strategies.

Attract Qualified Visitors

Taking traffic first, you can use the search engines to bring all sorts of visitors to your site, before, during and after your offline campaign. You can attract people asking for your product or asking for your brand, people who don't want to guess your URL and those who can't tell the difference between a browser and a search engine. You can catch people at all stages of the buying cycle, before they've even seen your promotion or when they're actively responding to your call to action.

You might be surprised to learn that the search engines are a useful part of your offline fulfilment. But even at the height of high profile advertising, dm or PR campaign, with a clearly marked URL or even a campaign-specific micro-site it doesn't matter how big or clever you make your call to action. You'd be amazed at the number of people who'll use search engines, rather than links, browsers, bookmarks, banners and buttons, to find what they're looking for. You can run a prime time TV campaign, with a celebrity footballer, whose name embodies the product, and a sizeable number of people will still go straight to a search engine and do a generic search, immediately after each ad is shown.

There are two choices, search engine optimization for the natural results and pay per click search engine marketing. Search engine optimization or SEO, is a long term strategy that involves re-engineering your site's structure, code and content to make it rich in the search terms your target audience is using and well connected to relevant sites. In essence, SEO can make sure that your web site's content, from your products and services, to your forums and bulletin boards, helps to make your site more search engine friendly. The alternative—and increasingly the complement—to SEO is Pay Per Click search engine marketing. You don't have to make any changes to your site and there are no ethical issues to contend with. If speed and flexibility are your priority, a Pay Per Click campaign can get your visibility off to a flying start, with traffic in just a couple of days.

Improve the Conversion Rate

So, now you've brought lots of qualified visitors to the site, as part of your fulfilment process. Next, how can your search engine marketing company help improve one of the key metrics by which the campaign will be measured, the conversion rate? After all, when you've invested in an offline campaign, you need to be certain that the web site can pick up the baton.

Fortunately, a good search engine marketing company will know how to make a web site visitor friendly, as well as search engine friendly.

— they'll look at how visitors are arriving at the site. Rather than just dropping people off at the home page and expecting them to find their own way from there, it's much better to take them straight to the content they're looking for. Campaign-specific micro-sites, with their own URL and dedicated content, often work well for this, plenty of respondents will use the search engines instead. So a good search engine marketing company will use deep linking strategies that connect your listings on the search engine results pages, whether natural or paid-for, to relevant content within your site.

— issue is the usability of the site. You can optimise the site to give your visitors a warm welcome and a smooth and seamless fulfilment service, from start to finish. Your search engine marketing company can make the site faster, smarter, friendlier and easier to use, with the navigation and content people are looking for, as part of its standard optimization service.

A good search engine marketing company can also make it accessible to all members of the online community, including those using assistive technologies, in accordance with the Disability Discrimination Act, which is promising to get tough about now. A good search engine marketing company will know exactly how to make your web site accessible—and will often include this as part of their standard optimization service.

Enhance and Protect Brand

Another vital contribution that your search engine

marketing company can make to your overall marketing strategy is that of enhancing and protecting your brand equity and integrity online. However well-known or well-regarded your brand offline, it is crucial that you are seen to own your brand on the search engines. After all, if you don't, someone else, with a potentially competitive or negative message such as a blogger, or forum posting, will take that space. There won't be a blank space in the search engine results page where you should rightfully be. Offline mindshare doesn't automatically deliver online equity, as several luxury brands have found to their cost.

A good search engine marketing company will ensure that you are in a highly visible position, not just under your company name, but your brands, products, services, trademarks and, just as importantly, promotional campaigns or creative straplines. This can be achieved either through the natural or paid-for results, depending on your budget, timescales and overall search engine marketing strategy.

Make yourself Heard

Audibility, as well as visibility, is a central part of a successful public relations strategy, and again, your search engine marketing company can add a lot of value. To start with, they can carry out keyword research to find out what kind of information people are looking for and define your news, product information and corporate messaging based on the search terms that people are using. As with profiling and targeting, search engine marketing intelligence turns the traditional communications paradigm on its head, because you're basing your strategy on what people want, rather than what you want to tell them. Likewise, they can ensure that your press releases and editorial features are search engine friendly, to ensure you can be easily found when people are looking for news on an ongoing basis, and position you as an authority in that space, which improves your link equity and therefore your visibility, at the same time. Vitally, your search engine marketing company can also help you provide a quick response to a sudden event or issue, control the messaging and hence protect your brand and market share.

Customer Relationship Management

Just as importantly, your search engine marketing company can help you get to know your current and potential customers in a completely new way—by providing vital intelligence for your CRM knowledge base. In practical terms, it's about offering privileges in return for information. People are quite happy to provide personal information about themselves in return for, say, an email newsletter, access to VIP content or to claim a special offer. Your search engine marketing company can set up your site to gather this information—with data capture opportunities at the front end, database integration at the back and cookies everywhere. In conjunction with visitor tracking, this data provides a wealth of intelligence to enable you to send out more targeted, personalised communications both offline and online.

Reporting

Finally, when you've run your offline campaign and you're reporting on the results, there are several ways your search engine marketing company can help—in a variety of formats and layouts. With access to your visitor tracking data, your search engine marketing company should be able to give you detailed information about your campaign, from the quantity of the response to the quality of the fulfilment process.

9 Internet Marketing Intelligence

Recently, numerous Internet-based business models have been developed, of which electronic commerce is playing a key role. The transition from vast amounts of Internet server and transaction data to actionable marketing intelligence is one of the major challenges in this research field.

The conglomerate of quasi standardised log file formats and highly domainspecific marketing data requires a holistic approach to collect, pre-process, and consolidate available web site information, in order to provide flexible materialised views for explorative operations such as online analytical processing or data mining (consequently named online analytical web usage mining).

Data Sources

We have developed an on-line retailing model, which contains the processes on an Internet retailer web site, as well as the back-end data storage components, which is depicted in Figure 1. The on-line retailing model is the permutation selected to research the efficacy of data mining.

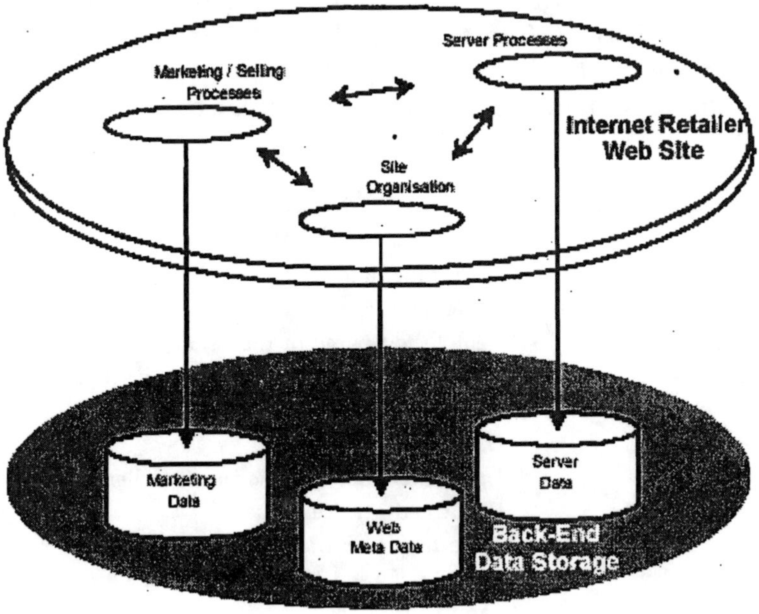

Figure 1. Online Retail Model

The primary reasons for selecting the on-line retailing model are behavioural (consumers exhibit a wide range of differing behavioural patterns), marketing-orientated (consumer and product information provides a rich source of useful data), and descriptive (products and services in on-line retail sites are varied).

Server Data

Server data is generated by the interactions between the persons browsing an individual site and the web server. The *httpd* process that runs on web servers provides a facility to log information on accesses to the server. That data can be divided into log files and query data. There are three types of log files, namely server logs, error logs, and cookie logs. Server logs are either stored in the

Common Logfile Format or the more recent Extended Logfile Format. The available field information from the two files is shown in Table 1, where the gray shaded cells indicate support in the extended format only.

Table 1. Server Log File Formats

Field	Description
date	Date, time, and timezone of request
client	IP Remote host IP and / or DNS entry
user name	Remote log name of the user
bytes	Bytes transferred (sent and received)
server	Server name, IP address and port
request	URI query and stem
status	*http* status code returned to the client
service name	Requested service name
time taken	Time taken for transaction to complete
protocol version	Version of used transfer protocol
user agent	Service provider
cookie	Cookie ID
referrer	previous page

Additionally, the Extended Logfile Format supports directives which provide meta information about the log file, such as version, start and end date of session monitoring, as well as the fields which are being recorded. Error logs store data of failed requests, such as missing links, authentication failures, or timeout problems. Apart from detecting erroneous links or server capacity problems - which, when satisfactorily corrected, can be seen as a compulsory form of customer satisfaction - the usage of error logs has proven to be rather limited for the discovery of actionable marketing intelligence.

Cookies are tokens generated by the web server and held by the clients. The information stored in a cookie log helps to ameliorate the transactionless state of web server interactions, enabling servers to track client access across their hosted web pages. The logged cookie data is customisable, which goes hand in hand with the structure and content of the marketing data.

A fourth data source that is typically generated on electronic commerce sites is query data to a web server. For example, customers to an online store may search for products, or clients to a research database may search for publications. The logged query data must be linked to the access log through cookie data and/or registration information. There are currently no formal drafts for standards for handling query data, although new specification suggestions have reached draft stage, for instance Resource Description Framework RDF.

Marketing Data and Knowledge

Any organisation that uses the Internet to trade in services and products uses some form of information system to operate Internet retailing. Clearly, some organisations use more sophisticated systems than others. The least common denominator information that is typically stored is about customers, products and transactions, each in different levels of detail. More sophisticated electronic traders keep also track of customer communication, distribution details, advertising information on their sites associated with products and / or services, sociographic information, and so forth.

A second type of information which is stored in modern environments is marketing knowledge. This type of domain expertise, obtained internally or externally, has usually been formulated by (human or artificial) marketing experts. It can be in the form of target-directed data collated from cross-fertilised sources, or the output of online analytical web mining activities carried out at an earlier stage. More formalised domain knowledge is expressed in hierarchical generalisation trees (for example, the topological organisation of Internet domains) or attribute relationship rules (marketing-specific constraints). The commonality of both sources is its arbitrary nature and hence structure, which has to be considered in each electronic commerce scenario.

Web Meta Data

The last source is data about the site itself, usually generated dynamically and automatically after a site update. Web meta data provides the topology of a site, which includes neighbour pages, leaf nodes and entry points. This information is usually implemented as site-specific index table, which represents a labelled directed graph. Meta data also provides information whether a page has been created statically or dynamically and whether user interaction is required or not.

In addition to the structure of a site, web meta data can also contain information of more semantic nature. Examples are arbitrary or ontology-based content information, usually represented through HTML meta tags or XML statements, the type of a page (root, navigational, content page, or a hybrid thereof), or page scores, which have been derived according to some pre-defined set of heuristics.

Data Preparation

This section deals with the data preparation of that information. The data preparation step contains two major tasks, namely the resolution of schematic and semantic heterogeneities among the relevant data, and a battery of pre-processing activities, some of which are generic, but most are Internet- and electronic commerce-specific.

Heterogeneity Resolution

Schematic heterogeneity

Due to the fact that most server data sources are standardised, relatively little schematic heterogeneity occurs in these files. Major discrepancies in log files are different physical arrangements of fields in server and error logs, and different field names recorded by different web servers. These naming mismatches are easily resolved using mapping files. These mapping files are either created manually or by (semi-)automated techniques as recommended in the literature. Cookie logs are either used to join various customer-related information sources or to identify reoccurring events. Depending on the structure of the cookie, the types of schematic heterogeneities that occur are naming conventions and different formats.

Naming conflicts are resolved analogous to incompatibilities in server and error log files; formatting conflicts are resolved using parameterised conversion functions. Cookies can only be handled in a canonical form if they have been set up with the intention to do so - there is no possibility to resolve schematic conflicts generically among different cookie types or dangling cookies. Less standardised and hence more unstructured is query data, since it is usually set up for individual, application- and domain-specific purposes.

Depending on the design and the pre-planned activities, the type of schematic heterogeneity is of differing granularity. Assuming that some form of planning has been performed, typical types of discrepancies are naming conflicts and data representation on domain level, and schema isomorphism on entity level (different number of attributes representing the query and its result). Similar to log files, domain level conflicts can be resolved using mappings and conversion functions;

deriving missing fields is the most common form to deal with schema isomorphism.

Similarly, type, content and structure of marketing information and meta data depend heavily on the electronic commerce domain, the topology of the site, the logical and physical interconnectivity with other sites (for instance on shopping malls), and so forth. Again, and ideally, in the case where the entire environment has been designed for the purpose of the collaboration of marketing and Internet data, the amount of schematic conflicts to resolve is minimal. But, more realistically, it is more likely that server and meta data has to be logically connected to an already existing marketing data pool.

The most typical discrepancies encountered are representation mismatches of marketing information (for instance customer numbers) and log files (cookie identifiers as well as the identification of a specific customer through standard log file information), and also between marketing data and meta data. Most inconsistencies are resolved through mapping tables, whereas some require further pre-processing..

Semantic heterogeneity

After the creation of a conflict-free schema, various interpretations of available data sources are necessary. Typical examples in log files are date and time formats of logs being used in different countries, query information in different languages, or URIs which are interpreted differently in different contexts, for example, the suffix .com might represent commercial organisations in one situation, whereas in another context it might include private users as well (for instance, customers who are logged in through a service provider). Similar scenarios exist in marketing as well as web meta data, especially when data is distributed across different locations.

There exist two general approaches of how to tackle semantic heterogeneity. One is a priori, which requires that the context in which the information will be used is known; the other one is a posteriori, which allows the usage of information in multiple contexts. In the context of web mining it is sufficient to follow the first direction, since the usage of the data - discovering marketing intelligence - is well defined, as opposed to running dynamic queries from multiple users against the collected data. Consequently, semantic heterogeneity can be resolved at the data pre-processing stage.

Pre-processing Activities

In addition to generic data warehousing-like preprocessing activities, some Internet- and electronic commerce-specific operations have to be carried out. First group consists of a set of techniques comprising cleaning, transforming, and aggregating.

From server logs, meta data files and some optional usage statistics, a user session file, a transaction file, the site topology, and page classifications are derived. Some activities are based on artificial intelligence techniques, for instance, the page classification is based on rule induction, whereas others use lookup tables, filtering (of multimedia information), and so on.

Many of the outlined pre-processing steps have been adopted, since they are inevitable for successful web usage mining. In order to handle all data sources as outlined in the previous section, essential operations were added. Some of the techniques were expanded in order to handle extended log file entries and customer data were linked to a user session via cookies. Furthermore, some initial work has been carried out in considering ontology-based content information, expressed in XML. Also, a new data type URL has been added to the data mining system MKS, which has been developed at the authors' laboratory.

A Materialised View

After a rather informal description of data sources in electronic commerce scenarios and an arsenal of heterogeneity resolution and pre-processing techniques, the physical and logical design of the data warehouse is presented more formally.

Web Log Data Hypercube

In order to create a materialised view which is used as repository for further analytical activities, an ndimensional web log data cube is defined. A web log data hypercube *H* represents an n-dimensional information space, such that $H = [D_1, D_2, D_3, \ldots, D_n]$, where each D_x represents a dimension of *H*. This hypercube represents an intentionally denormalised materialised view of the pre-processed data.

A dimension D_x represents m attributes such that $D_x = [a_{x1}, a_{x2}, a_{x3}, \ldots, a_{xm}]$. Some attributes may be derived fields in order to hold summarisation information, like resource hits, sales aggregation, or customer purchase sums.

The total number of cells is calculated as $|C| = \prod_{i=1}^{n} |H_i|$

where $|H_i|$ is the cardinality of *H* (number of attributes). This number leads to an exponential growth of the number of cells, many of which are naturally sparse, which is handled by internal compression mechanism. Also, efficient computation of the web hypercube has to be guaranteed.

In order to simplify generalisation and aggregation operations as well as the modelling of dimensional hierarchies in snowflake schemas, each dimension is defined on a multi-level concept hierarchy.

A concept hierarchy T is an undirected, connected, acyclic graph which is defined as the tuple $T = (L, E)$, where $L = \{l_0, l1_1, l1_2, ..., l_1|l1|, l2_1, l2_2, ..., l_2|l_2|, ..., l_{n1}, l_{n2}, ..., l_n|l_n|\}$ and $E = \{e_1, e_2, e_3, ..., e_m\}$.

Each l_x represents a value of a domain D_x of a hypercube *H*, such that the granularity $g(l_n) < g(l_{n-1})$, $n > 0$. Each ek has the form $e_k = \{l_i, l_j\}; l_i, l_j \in L$, l0 has indegree 0, l1...ln have indegree 1. l_i is subconcept of $l_j \subset i_{ff}$ *li lj; li* is superconcept of l_j *iff lj* $\subset$ *li*.

Thus, a hypercube can also be represented as an ntuple $H=(T_1, T_2, T_3, ..., T_n)$. An example of a threedimensional web log data cube as well as a drilleddown version with the dimensions customer, location and product is depicted in Figure 2.

Schematic Design

To construct a cube as depicted above and supporting further analysis activities such as OLAP and data mining, a schema based on the relational calculus is modelled. Each dimension is represented as a relation, which is connected to a fact table. Fact tables act as connecting element in a data model representing keys and summarisation information. This star schema is sufficient for one given set of scenarios, which uses data input of the same granularity. For more advanced operations, as necessary in web mining, a snowflake schema is required, which supports multiple granularities. Snowflake schemas provide a refinement of star schema where the dimensional hierarchy is explicitly represented by normalising dimension tables.

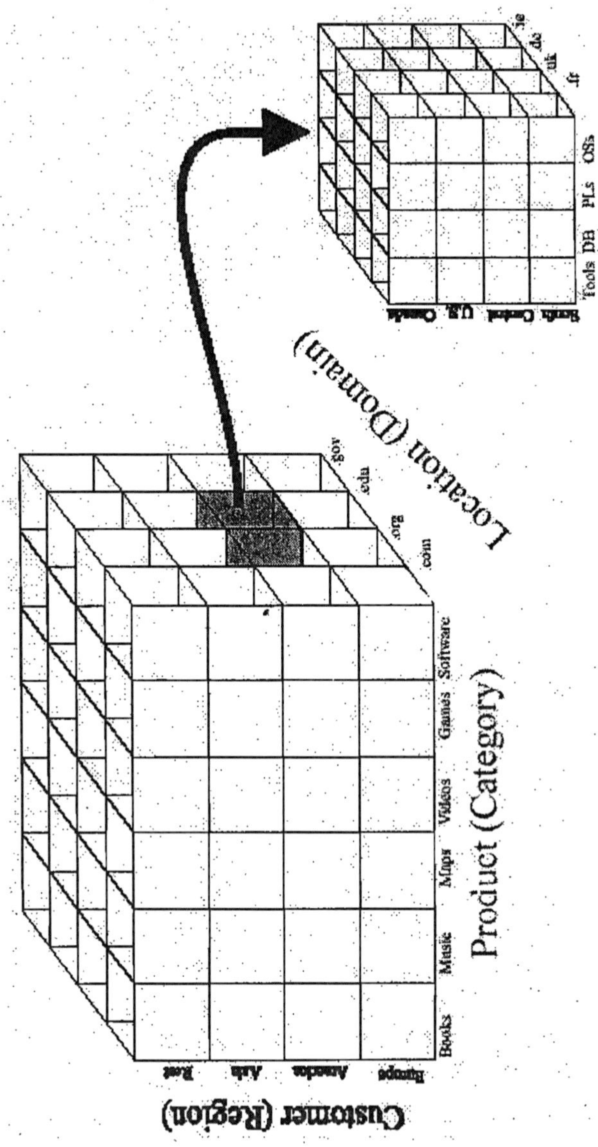

Figure 2. A three-dimensional Web Log Data Cube

<u>CustomerKey</u>
<u>ProductKey</u>
<u>LocationKey</u>
<u>DateKey</u>
<u>SessionKey</u>
Quantity
TotalPrice
ClickThroughRate

Figure 3. A Web Log Fact Table

The following figure shows a fact table which is typical for analysis activities in electronic commerce scenarios. It contains key fields as well as some statistical summarisation information. Around this fact table it is now possible to create a star schema, which is used for simple analysis activities, as well as a basis for the more complex and powerful snowflake schema below. Although expressive enough for simple data analysis activities, the star schema is insufficient for complex web usage mining. A more flexible schema is provided below.

The snowflake schema depicted above is just one possible example, which can be used to handle data from Internet sources. Other alternatives are possible, depending on the problem to be solved.

Marketing Intelligence

In order to facilitate the steps carried out above, a web-enabled knowledge discovery process has been developed (Figure 6), which is an adoption of a generic process defined in earlier work. The process contains the entire life-cycle of a knowledge discovery project and involves

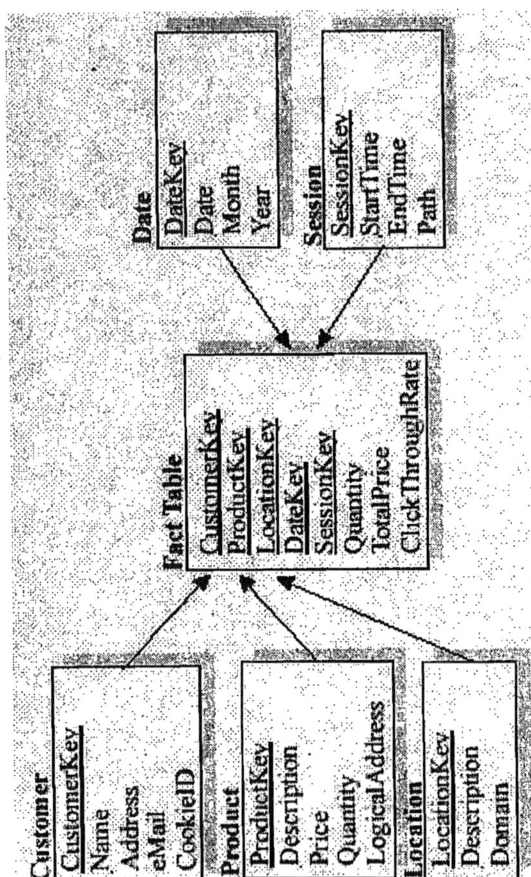

Figure 4. A Web Log Star Schema

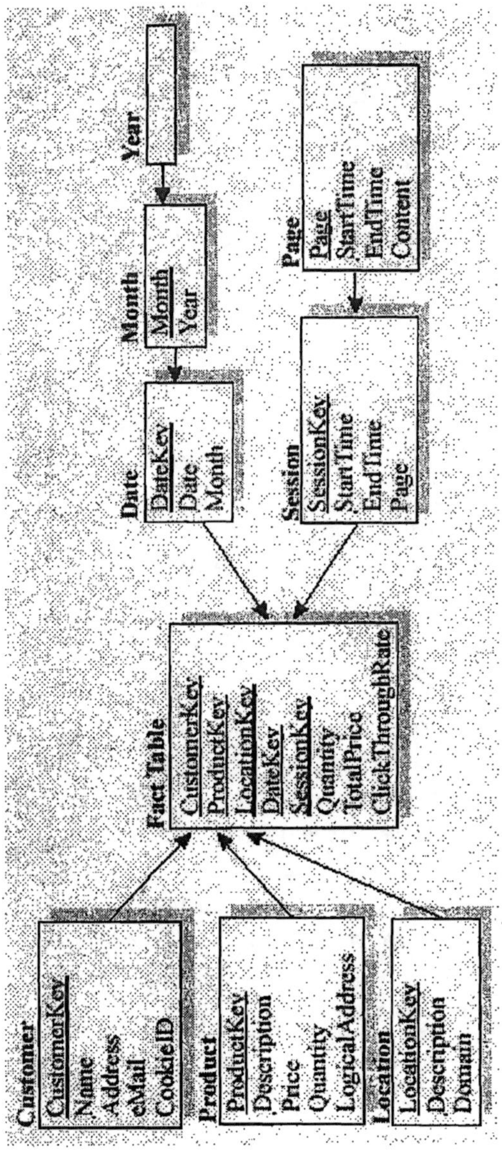

Figure 5. A Web Log Snowflake Schema

required expertise, personified as a web administrator, a marketing expert, and a data mining expert, all of whom are involved in various steps of the process.

Marketing experts divide the customer relationship life-cycle into three distinct steps, which cover attraction, retention, and cross-sales. A pattern discovery scenario is presented for each period, each of which covers the discovery goal, marketing strategy, and data mining approach.

Customer Attraction

The two essential parts of attraction are the selection of new prospective customers and the acquisition of the selected potential candidates. One marketing strategy to perform this exercise, among others, is to find common characteristics in already existing visitors' information and behaviour for the classes of profitable and non-profitable customers. These groups are then used as labels for a classifier to discover Internet marketing rules, which are applied online on new site visitors.

Depending on the outcome, a dynamically created page is displayed, whose contents depends on found associations between browser information and offered products / services. The three classification labels used were 'no customer', that is browsers who have logged in, but did not purchase, 'visitor once' and 'visitor regular'. An example rule is as follows.

```
if Region = IRL and
   Domain1 IN [uk, ie] and
   Session > 320 Seconds
then VisitorRegular
Support = 6,4%; Confidence = 67,2%
```

This type of rule can then be used for further marketing actions such as displaying special offers to first time browsers from the two mentioned domains after they have spent a certain period of time on the shopping site.

Customer Retention

Customer retention or attrition is the step of attempting to keep the online shopper as loyal as possible. Due to the non-existence of distances between providers, this is an extremely challenging task in electronic commerce scenarios. One strategy is similar to that of acquisition, that is dynamically creating web offers based on associations. However, it has been proven more successful to consider associations across time, also known as sequential patterns. Typical sequences in electronic commerce data are representing navigational behaviour of shoppers in the forms of page visit series.

A found sequence looks as following.

```
{
ecom.infm.ulst.ac.uk/,
ecom.infm.ulst.ac.uk/News_Resources.html,
ecom.infm.ulst.ac.uk/Journals.html,
ecom.infm.ulst.ac.uk/,
ecom.infm.ulst.ac.uk/search.htm,
}
Support = 3.8%; Confidence = 31.0%
```

The discovered sequence can then be used to display special offers dynamically to keep a customer interested in the site, after a certain page sequence with a threshold support and / or confidence value has been visited.

Cross-Sales

The objective of cross-sales is to horizontally and / or vertically diversify selling activities to an existing customer base. A traditional crosssales methodology, in order to perform the given task in an electronic commerce environment. In order to discover potential customers, characteristic rules of existing cross-sellers had to be discovered, which was performed through the application of attribute-orientated induction. For a scenario in which the product CD is being cross-sold to book sellers, an example rule is

```
if Product = book then
   Domain1 = uk and
   Domain2 = ac and
   Category = Tools
Support = 16.4%; Interest = 0.34
```

Deviation detection is used to calculate the interest measure and to filter out the less interesting rules. The entire set of discovered interesting rules can then be used as the model to be applied at run-time on incoming actions and requests from existing customers.

10

Measuring Marketing Effectiveness

What good is marketing without measurement? You need a way to sift through reams of customer interactions for accurate reporting and analysis—but with so much intricate data available, it's possible to lose sight of the big picture. Join us to learn best practices for measuring marketing effectiveness and return.

Data Integration

Bringing together data from disparate systems has always been difficult. With the advent of the Internet and XML, expectations have grown exponentially. As the Web and e-commerce have lowered the cost and the technical pain associated with EDI (electronic data interchange) between companies, need to lower the cost and technical pain of acquiring data from disparate systems within the organisation and display that data in a usable way.

Individual systems have certainly been providing valuable information:

— Marketing Automation systems data can reveal.

  — Comparative media cost effectiveness.

  — Comparative message effectiveness.

- Sales tracking software can indicate.
  - Sales representative productivity.
  - Average customer conversion/time-to-close ratios.
- Customer Relationship Management data can divulge.
  - . Customer retention and loyalty statistics.
  - Customers profitability metrics.
- Web Analytics software can show.
  - Depth of prospect interest.
  - Prospect response to messaging.
- Support data can provide.
  - Profiles on typical customer problems.
  - Preferred methods of support delivery.

However, when information from all of these sources is integrated, new depths of marketing process visibility impart more valuable and more actionable insights:

- Which promotions produced the most qualified leads.
- Which promotions resulted in the most revenue.
- Which products are the most profitable .

Automating the integration of this information is key to making it useful. Placing data visualisation tools into the hands of front-line decision makers will make the information actionable. Using XML, Web Services, self-describing data marts and the Internet, now create a tool set that will swiftly and efficiently gather and integrate the most useful information, and display it through a exceptionally understandable interface. Given this access to the data, the next step is to clearly specify the information we want.

Performance Indicators

Measuring marketing performance has always been a challenge due to our inability to fathom which metrics are meaningful. We now have the ability to capture data elements from almost every stage of the persuasion process from awareness to satisfaction. As a result, making the identification of meaningful data overwhelming. Key performance indicators for marketing vary according to specific areas of responsibility. Following the path of awareness to satisfaction and loyalty, metrics for the following areas of responsibility:

— Brand Manager.

— Product Marketing Manager.

— Public Relations Manager.

— Business Development Manager.

— Advertising Manager.

— Promotion & Lead Generation Manager.

— Web Site Manager.

— Sales Manager.

— Customer Relationship Manager.

Role of Brand Manager

While internal processes generate ad capture data as a matter of course, the figures necessary to gauge the success of a brand are derived from outside research. This data is usually gathered by hand and stored in a report or a spreadsheet. Provided this information remains in a constant format, it can be extracted for inclusion in a dashboard report. Starting with a descriptive, static metric of brand equity, the data becomes informative when plotted over time. The brand manger can track the rise and fall of the company's or product's stature and forecast the future potential of brand equity over time. Brand managers need to stay on top of the shifts in statistics such as *brand equity , brand awareness, brand preference, brand image, and brand loyalty.*

Role of Product Marketing Manager

Product marketing managers spend half their time in manufacturing and half in marketing. There are many systems to inform this individual about the development and production process, but few to reveal progress on the marketing side. Like the brand manager, the product marketing manager is focused on customer opinion. Should we add new features? Should we raise or lower the price? Product marketing managers will keep an eye on all of the aforementioned brand-related gauges, as well as sales and customer satisfaction survey results. They will want to take action based on reports of *customer satisfaction, market share, price sensitivity, over all sales and sales by channel.*

Role of Public Relations Manager

Clipping services often provide the PR department with the information they want most: *media mentions.* How often did the company "get ink"? This numeric accounting of public exposure includes weighting those appearances by the size of the audience. A write-up in the local newspaper's business section doesn't carry as much *visibility* as an interview on CNN. The positive or negative nature of those occurrences are also considered when judging the success of a PR project or individual.

Role of Business Development Manager

The role of the business development manager varies widely but is primarily responsible for partnerships with other companies. These other firms might be part of the distribution chain or cooperative marketing partners. They might be direct sales organisations or manufacturers that use components or sub-assemblies in their systems offerings.

The accomplishments of the business development manager can be quantified by measuring *partner acquisition per month , partner participation per month, partner turnover/ churn.* Acquisition and loss speak for themselves, but acquiring partners may not be in the best interest of the company if those partners do not participate in trade shows, advertising, sales, or whatever other activity in which they are signed up to engage. *Sales by channel* is the easiest number to glean from the accounting databases for those development managers responsible for value-added-resellers and multiple -level supply chains.

Role of Advertising Manager

The advertising world has been statistically oriented since its inception. *Reach* and *frequency* are the life blood of the advertising manager. How many potential ad viewers did we reach and how often? Multiply the two together and you have *gross rating points. Recall* relates whether those viewers remembered the ad and the *carryover effect* measures how the effectiveness of an advertising campaign diminishes over time. Specialised software applications allow advertisers to catalog and track these types of numbers. These statistics become extremely useful for the rest of the marketing organisation when they are extracted and integrated with the larger marketing picture.

- Brand managers need to keep track of message timing.
- Product marketing managers have to gauge prospect reactions.

— Public relations managers should orchestrate press releases with advertising.

— Business development managers can tip off partners of upcoming advertisements.

— Promotion and lead generation managers must coordinate ads with other promotions.

— Web site managers ought to be prepared for a large influx of visitors.

— Sales managers can juggle resources in the field.

— Customer relationship managers have to administer call centers.

Role of Promotion and Lead Generation Manager

Companies are closely scrutinising the return on investment for direct mail, seminars, telemarketing, and a myriad of other methods of lead generation. There are many ways to spend marketing dollars and knowing which programmes generate leads is no longer enough. While advertising is still a little too far from the sale to be tightly linked, lead generators are under pressure to produce not just more leads, but better leads. This means they are using systems that follow each lead through the sales cycle. They watch each lead that comes in to see how well qualified it is and whether it turned into a sale. The *leads to closing ratio* will disclose which promotions are worth repeating.

Role of Web Site Manager

The Web site manager lives in a separate realm of Web metrics. These numbers help determine the validity of the Web site navigation and design, the efficacy of content choices and the health of the technology that supports the site.

Role of Sales Manager

Sales managers live and breath sales figures. Comparative sales across regions, sales forecasts by sales representative, sales of ancillary products or supplies are all part of their daily input. This information is crucial for marshalling sales resources, adjusting territories, and figuring out how to squeeze every last dollar out of a month.

Sales managers have long lived with these numbers as they are part and parcel of the accounting system. Orders get booked, invoices get sent, commissions get paid. Sales forces quickly discovered the power of contact management systems. Those contacts can now become a visible part of the marketing process and vice versa. An ad campaign or a promotion can trigger a flurry of sales calls, with the results fed back into the lead management system.

Role of Customer Relationship Manager

Customer relationship management (CRM) is the gathering and leveraging of information about customers rather than about manufacturing and accounting processes. Likes and dislikes, the best time to contact, buying authority, influence within an organisation and more are the keys to knowing customers one-to-one.

Those responsible for CRM all face the task of information extraction and integration; sometimes through large, expensive projects and sometimes with a number of small applications. There is no CRM finish line or "total solution." There is only the constant and growing gathering of information and trying to make it actionable. In the case of CRM, the actions take the form of customer segmentation, customer privileges, and customer recognition in order to improve satisfaction and, therefore, increase sales.

The majority of CRM systems are being used in an insulated manner. They are performing their functions as programmed, but have not widely reached their potential of delivering knowledge that can be used to fuel insight. There is still a need to access CRM systems' data, integrate it with other marketing process management systems, and produce a display/dashboard/live report that can be manipulated to inspire intuition.

Responsibility of Marketing Executives

Overall responsibility resides with the Chief Marketing Executive. One hopes that a human with sufficient years of experience and ample intelligence can hold a wide variety of disparate concepts, beliefs and facts in mind while ruminating over the costs and benefits of various strategic choices. With the proper information extracted, gathered, and integrated, the executive can now conceive, believe and ruminate with facts that are as far flung as possible and as close to real time as possible.

Product marketing managers want visibility over which promotions garner the best results for the lowest cost. In turn, marketing executives want visibility over which departments are getting the best results for the money. The executive should be the conveyor of new ideas, breakthrough results and best practices between all of the marketing managers. What Key Performance Indicators are valuable this high up in the chain of command?

- — Leads generated per dollar spent by department
- — Sales per dollar spent by department
- — Length of sales cycle by department
- — Change in brand awareness and attitude by department

Once the critical metrics have been selected, the next challenge is to display the figures in the most decipherable manner. The goal is to have a dashboard that is easy to interpret, allowing ·displayed results to be actionable as quickly as possible.

Effect of Information Crystallisation and Display

The visual display of complex data doesn't depend on new metaphors or 3-D glasses. Business decision makers will succeed when they can understand the displayed information at a glance and quickly modify the variables they are studying. There are two secrets to making data actionable. First, anomalies must be instantly recognisable and then the reports must be malleable; the manager at the monitor must be able to sort, model, monitor, compare and drill in order to satisfy intuition, rather than merely respond to stimulus.

Most managers are still drawing data from multiple sources, importing it into Excel for number crunching and then outputting it to PowerPoint for distribution. A high value, low cost, low risk application is needed to gather, model and analyse the data to support the decision making process. This application must ensure that all players are looking at and working with the same data at the same time.

While decision making using common data is critical, providing discretionary views of information helps an organisation leverage each managers cognitive skills. Managers do not give the same weight to the same information. Each has his or her own perspective. When given the ability to manipulate information in an intuitive manner, they can follow a hunch to gain insight.

Except in the largest organisations, this has not been possible due to the effort necessary to regenerate a new configuration of variables. A manager wanting to compare two sales representatives' progress by size of proposal during a period of time probably has that report on hand. But should that manager want to contrast that progress on a year over year basis, or compare them based on length of sales cycle, chances are excellent the impulse will be suppressed due to the exertion required to describe, define, format, extract and deliver such a report.

Rather than creating engineering specifications so the fabrication team can manufacture a prototype, the manager can work more intuitively with a handful of clay. A visually oriented, mutable data display application lets the manager manipulate the information as quickly as she thinks. With enough reporting variety, the data can fit the pattern of her thoughts in real time. This would be a system that makes the computer do the work to meet the needs of the human, rather than make the human cater to the idiosyncrasies of the computer.

Managers would be able to reach into the datamart, identify the data they wish to work with, select the style of chart or graph they wish to see, break the information down by subset, aggregate it by series, filter it by sundry criteria, and save the result as a view they wish to monitor.

If the system responds rapidly enough, it can be used as a planning tool during meetings.

— "Look at how well Susan is doing with the $25,000 contracts while Fred is going gangbusters with the $15,000 deals."

— "Let's see how that breaks down across vertical markets."

— "Are they both keeping up with their quota goals?"

— "Drop in their pipeline numbers. Are they both prospecting the same across all opportunities?"

— "It looks we should get the two of them in here to give a workshop to the rest of the team on how they're making these sales."

11

Ethical Marketing for Competitive Advantage on the Internet

Marketing practice is now busy integrating the potential of information and communication technologies through the utilisation of databases and Internet marketing. Billions of potential consumers can now be reached this way. Nevertheless, a brief observation of the practices of marketing on the Internet show that some firms implement aggressive actions such as pop-ups, deceiving banners and hyperlinks and other forms of intrusive mechanisms which impinge on personal privacy. As technology moves from desk based PC applications to mobile communications, there is potential to become even more intrusive, with the possibility of local tracking. The model of ethical interactivity seven types of practice such as notice, choice, access, contact, security, horizon, and intrusiveness. Correct interpretation of these practices leads to empowered consumers creating greater benefits for the firm and for the consumers themselves.

Ethical Marketing Practices

The observation of marketing practice on the Internet can give an idea of the types of unethical practices that are either already in place or recommended by certain marketing consultancy sites. A simple analysis of many sites highlights two important issues. The first one is concerned with the gathering of consumer information and the second one is concerned with the utilisation of various marketing techniques. These are many and varied ranging from banners to fixed spot advertisements and flash advertisements and the selling or exchange of consumer information.

Gathering Information and Issue of Consumer Information Privacy

As Kelly notes, Internet technology provides opportunities to gather consumer information "on an unprecedented scale". However some aspects of information gathering are visible and some are less visible. Owing to these possible uses and abuses of information, many consumers remain hesitant about Internet purchasing. The development of software allowing "private Internet experience" and 'completely undetected surfing' is an indication of consumer concern regarding the invasion of privacy. A survey of the top 100 commercial web sites shows that only 20 per cent apply a full ethical policy. This shows that there is room for the development of competitive advantage. Culnan's reports on Internet privacy policy show that five aspects can used to describe a web site's position concerning privacy:

— *Notice:* that is an indication to the consumer about what information is collected, how it will be used; whether is will be disclosed to third parties and whether cookies are used or not.

— *Choice:* is the consumer given the choice to agree with aspects of information gathering?

— *Access:* does the consumer have access to the information gathered? Is the consumer given the possibility and correct the information?

— *Security* :concerns the protection of information transfer and subsequent storage.

— *Contact:* are consumers given a contact person or address for asking questions or registering complaints regarding privacy?

Marketing Tools on the Internet

Advertising is an important marketing tool on the Internet with a range of possibilities for customer interactivity and involvement. Banner advertising has been an important vehicle for many Internet based advertisements with much research dedicated to its design elements. At the same time, marketing professionals try to understand how individuals surf through websites and consequently attempt to increase the CTR (click-through ratio). In this respect, researchers as well as practitioners try to identify key variables: type and size of ad banners, animation, use of colour, sounds, images, incentives, etc. Certain practices can be observed and are recommended as efficient ones: pop-ups, deceiving banners. Here are some excerpts from the advice given for designing an efficient banner:

— Feature a Call To Action,

— Create Urgency,

— Use the Word "FREE,"

— Certain truisms remain true-intrigue and sex sell

Parallel to Internet advertising, the development of e-mail marketing and spam are features of aggressive e-marketing.

Ethical Nature of Marketing Practices

In the field of advertising, Nwachukwu et al. found that three variables are important for judging the ethical nature of an ad: individual autonomy, consumer sovereignty and harmfulness of product. These ideas are utilised to assess specific ads and to assess sovereignty in terms of consumer awareness of a product's use and availability.

Individual autonomy refers to the ability of the individual to recognise the manipulative power of advertising. Consumer sovereignty refers to the level of knowledge and sophistication of the target audience. Lastly, harmfulness of product refers to the nature of the product. On the Internet, harmfulness could be defined by the advertising of pornography or harmful visual imagery.

Other aspects that surely need to be considered in Internet advertising are the levels of ad intrusiveness and personal privacy. Some areas of Internet advertising compare with general advertising tactics.

Some light on how advertising on the Internet can impinge on customer autonomy and sovereignty by being intrusive and disrespectful of personal privacy. If consider the key factors pointed out by Nwachukwu et. al., take into account Culnan's criteria of online privacy and add intrusiveness to the mix, it is possible to create a model for understanding and judging ethical marketing practices on the Internet. This model is illustrated in Figure 1.

The model shows how individual autonomy, consumer sovereignty and harmfulness of product interact with the seven factors that are shown. The composite of seven factors in addition to Culnan's factors of notice, choice, contact, security and access, include horizon and intrusiveness. The time element, in terms of how long companies can access customer information is important as is the degree of intrusiveness.

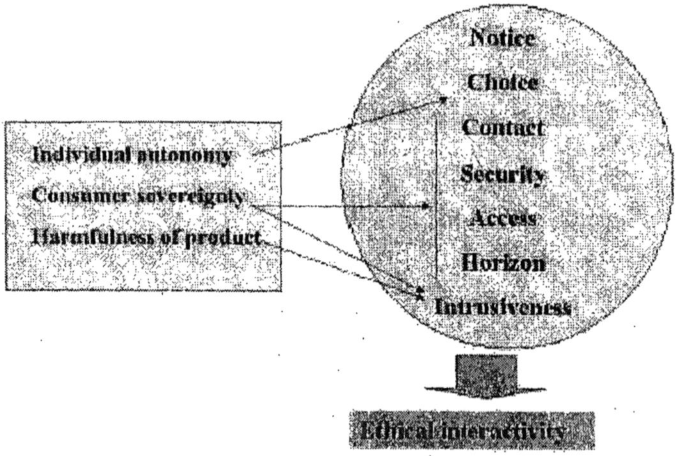

Figure 1 Delineating Ethical Internet Marketing

These seven factors could be used to evaluate the overall degree of ethical interactivity of a company on the Internet. A zero level ethical stance corresponds to an offer of notice and security However, as noted by Culnan, the level of disclosure can range from a comprehensive privacy policy notice (PPN) to a discrete statement. This might be difficult to provide as customer details can be either gathered from the home page or through hyperlinks to the home page. Nonetheless, paying attention to these two factors show the degree of ethical concern afforded to the consumer by a company.

A comprehensive PPN linked from the homepage and the highest level of security are the minimal level that firms should aspire to in order to exhibit a reasonable degree of ethical behaviour on the Internet. However, this may not be entirely sufficient and a higher levels of ethical interactivity should also be considered by most firms.

Higher levels of ethical interactivity can be offered by a serious consideration of the five other criteria, which are choice, contact, access, horizon, intrusiveness. Each of these in its own right helps to improve the levels of ethical interactivity undertaken by a firm.

All these factors help to create *consumer empowerment*. Not only should consumers be given the chance to self disclose private information, they should also be given the opportunity to clearly and precisely agree on the manner in which it will be used. In particular, the level of intrusiveness of marketing techniques could be agreed upon, as some consumers are open to a variety of techniques, looking at them as sources of information. However in some cases, intrusions may simply be considered to be fun, such as the viral marketing strategy adopted for a computer game. For others an official letter of introduction may be the only way forward. Consumers should also be made aware of the frequency of contact, choosing their own level frequency. The horizon criterion relates to the time frame in which the information will be utilised. Here again, consumers could choose to receive marketing incentives for either a short or a long period of time. Finally, the possibility of anonymous visits to a website, free of any tracking could also be offered.

Leveraging the degree of ethical interactivity will help to tailor marketing actions according to *consumer ethical flexibility*. The ethical sensitivity of a consumer could even become a *segmentation criterion*. This is all the more important than ethical sensitivity is likely to differ from one sector to another, just as Nwachukwu et al. noted about certain products like cigarettes. Also, for instance, consumers could be less ethically sensitive when buying a book and far more ethically sensitive when using online banking.

Ethics of E-Marketing

Singhapakdi showed that marketing managers who perceive an ethical problem in a situation are more likely to have an ethical intention. Hence, marketing professionals engage in more thought and reflect on their marketing practices on the Internet. This could lead to a greater consciousness and hence to the development of more ethical intentions and practices. The question of adopting an ethical marketing behaviour does not only boil down to providing a firm's policy concerning information privacy, it should also be demonstrated in marketing actions. The seven criteria presented above can serve as a guideline for firms wanting to implement an ethical e-marketing strategy. Survey of other web sites practices can also help. For instance, in France, the site Voilà.fr decided to ban the use of "pop-ups", as this was deemed too aggressive for Internet users.

The comfort of secure navigation is a key to internet-user satisfaction, the absence of intrusive techniques can be part of this comfort and hence lead to consumer satisfaction and loyalty. The design of the web site is often mainly evaluated in terms of pleasure and interactivity. It should integrate ethical considerations. Avoiding misleading, deceiving signs, controlling the ad banners that appears and preventing other intrusive advertising will be important in the future. It will also be important to inform consumers that a particular firm takes an ethical stance through the creation and diffusion of Internet ethical charts. Chonko and Hunt deplore the lack of ethical guidelines in marketing practices, however such a development and its diffusion to consumers will be critical in the future.

Both the deontological and utilitarian views of ethics can be used to design ethical web-sites. Whether any practices should be banned on the Internet, within a free society is a moot point. However, it is possible for firms to exercise self-restraint and also develop personalised sites that depend on each individual's tolerance levels. As Internet software becomes more sophisticated, it will be increasingly possible to tailor sites for individual ethical preferences. The seven criteria mentioned above could form the basis of creating and sustaining competitive advantages.

12

Successful E-mail Marketing Practices

Email marketing is one of the most successful and cost-effective ways to keep in touch with customers—by creating brand awareness, building customer loyalty, and driving sales. Companies expend a lot of effort building customer lists for email campaigns. It's frustrating, then, when more than 20 percent of legitimate email industry-wide never hits the inbox. But marketers can take proactive measures to improve the chances their emails will be delivered. The following five steps can immediately increase any organisation's open and response rates:

— Ask to be added to the address book

— Maintain consistent "from" information:

— Permission and recognition minimize complaints:

— Monitor content:

— Use a trusted sender:

Fast Facts

— Forty-five percent of Americans now use e-mail, a 10 percent increase since 2000 - U.S. Department of Commerce, February 2002.

— There are 95 million e-mail users in Europe holding about 200 million e-mail accounts - Forrester, October 2001.

— About 1.5 billion e-mail messages are sent per day in the United States, nearly three times the volume of direct mail pieces delivered daily by the USPS - eMarketer, May 2001.

— The average cost per message of opt-in e-mail is $.20, significantly cheaper than telemarketing or direct mail - eMarketer, May 2001.

— E-mail marketing messages are sent at a cost of $5 to $7 per thousand while direct mailings cost $500 to $700 per thousand -eMarketer, August 2002.

— Eighty percent of e-mail marketing message responses come back within 48 hours, as compared with the 6-8 week period for traditional direct marketing methods - Jupiter Research, May 2001.

— Permission-based e-mail generates click-through rates (CTR) ten times greater than that of banner advertising eMarketer, May 2001

— Three out of five consumers prefer text-only formatted e-mail ads over HTML or rich media-based e-mail - eMarketer, August 2002

E-Mail Marketing Benefits

E-mail is far less expensive on a cost per contact basis than other advertising options, including banner ads, print advertising and telemarketing. Thirty-five percent of Association for Interactive Marketing (AIM) member companies report that the cost of sending a single B2C e-mail marketing message is less than 1 cent.

E-mail cuts response times down from as much as six to eight weeks for direct mail to as little as 48 hours in most cases. Campaign success can be measured using software designed to record responses or sales that are attributable to e-mail marketing efforts. Reports can be generated on the number of e-mails opened by your recipients and the number of times your embedded links were clicked. By being able to quantify the success of campaigns while in progress, marketers can quickly adjust strategies to strengthen response rates.

E-mail is the most widely used facet of the Internet and is part of many people's daily routine. It is a communication medium with an exceptionally large audience that allows recipients to immediately act on messages. E-mail is an effective way of driving recipients to your Web site. Links may be embedded within messages, quickly directing customers to your site. With any luck, this increased Web site traffic will then lead to increased Web site registration. You may then follow up by providing your customers with personalised and targeted content.

Regularly delivered e-mail messages that contain properly titled subject lines and logos reinforce company and product awareness. Marketers are 10 times more likely to cite branding over lead capturing as a goal of an online campaign. E-mail creates an interactive connection with customers and nurtures long-lasting, quality relationships.

When e-mail lists work together with customer databases, even largevolume campaigns can be customised so that messages include specific customer data. Database integration also allows select customer groups to receive messages appropriate for only a portion of database entries. E-mail campaigns can be quickly implemented and executed with only minimal software, hardware and personnel investments.

Value of E-mail

Let's take into consideration this situation: Your company is planning to distribute a newsletter to customers, prospects and other interested parties, and it is your job to decide how to accomplish this task. The monthly newsletter will contain many regular features, including articles, advice and industry news. You have two options to distribute the newsletter: You can print the newsletter and snail-mail it to recipients—after all, this is how company newsletters have been distributed for many years. This is still an effective option, but you may not have realised many of the benefits of sending your newsletter via e-mail.

If you choose to e-mail the newsletter and select an advanced software programme to manage the mailing, you will be able to measure what sections of the newsletter are most popular with readers. When you send an e-mail newsletter, recipients click on embedded links to retrieve articles they wish to read. These clicks are measurable and provide you with valuable information that can, in turn, be used to tailor future newsletters to best suit readers' interests.

Market with E-Mail

As e-mail has evolved, marketers have discovered clever ways to take advantage of its usefulness. Some common ways companies have integrated e-mail into their communication efforts:

Inform IT, a subsidiary of Pearson Education that provides an online resource for technology information, uses LISTSERV® Maestro to deliver more than 20 newsletters to Web site members about topics ranging from programming to networking. These newsletters have enabled Inform IT to build a strong IT community that subscribers can depend on for up-to-date technology news.

Consulting firm InterImage was selected by the U.S. Department of Commerce's Minority Business Development Agency to develop an effective method to market the agency's annual conference. InterImage chose LISTSERV® Maestro's hosting alternative to administer five mailings to 137,000 opt-in recipients with the goal of increasing awareness for the event. After the initial mailing, the agency received 45,000 unique Web hits and is experiencing higher registration rates than in past years.

British Airways maintains more than 70 LISTSERV® lists. Currently, the airline is focused on furthering the development of its customer relationships. British Airways has recently been running targeted personalised campaigns offering customers special discounts and promotions. So far, these e-mails have proven popular with recipients.

As a free service to its community of women, in 1999 Lifetime TV launched the Lifetime Breast Self Examination Reminder Service to raise public awareness of breast cancer and the importance of early detection. Visitors to Lifetime TV's Web site are given the opportunity to register for monthly examination e-mail reminders. Since its creation, the Breast Self Examination Reminder list has been a tremendous success. Today, the subscriber base of the LISTSERV® list is 61,000.

In an effort to make billing information more accessible to customers, Bell Canada, the country's largest telephone company, decided to offer a service called Bill Viewing. Monthly e-mails that included a link to billing information were sent to customers who had subscribed to the service. The monthly billing notifications also served as an effective marketing tool for the company by providing links to special promotional offers and other incentives. In the three years Bell Canada has offered Bill

Viewing, the subscriber base of the company's LISTSERV® lists has steadily risen to 300,000.

SUCCESSFUL E-MAIL MARKETING CAMPAIGNS FOUR STEPS

List of Subscribers

In order to begin any e-mail marketing campaign, you must first compile a list of e-mail addresses from those who have agreed to receive your messages. This is known as opt-in e-mail marketing and is a very important part of your campaign. eMarketer reported in May 2001 that only 6 percent of permission-based e-mail is deleted unopened, while 59 percent of opt-out e-mail is deleted unopened.

Building a quality permission-based e-mail list will save you time and achieve more desirable results. When compiling these lists be sure to make your privacy policy clear to your subscribers. Be upfront about how secure your subscriber's information is, whether or not you will be sharing that information with a 3rd party, and specific instructions on how your subscribers can opt out of your list. So, with those concerns out of the way, where do you begin? A logical place to start gathering addresses is with:

— Current Customers who may have previously provided you their e-mail addresses and given you permission to send messages. Depending on how your business operates, there may be opportunities to collect your customers' e-mail addresses through purchase orders or other forms.

— Prospective Customers whose e-mail addresses may be obtained through sign-ups on your Web site or in-store locations. Advanced e-mail list management software has the ability to interact with your Web site so visitors may automatically subscribe to newsletters without your having to perform this function manually.

— List Brokers companies that specialise in compiling opt-in e-mail lists. However, please remember to follow the old adage, "buyer beware!" when choosing to take this route. Some list brokers sell unsubstantiated or unusable addresses.

Content and Format of Your Message Development

Messages should be crafted according to the results you wish to achieve. What are your goals for this campaign? Generating sales? Branding? Driving site traffic? Generally, you should create a strong message that reinforces your brand, describes your products or services and clearly establishes how customers should contact you. The subject line is possibly the most important element of an e-mail message. Create a powerful subject line by combining an action phrase with a response-boosting incentive. An example of a good subject line would be: Last Minute Fare Specials for Weekend Getaway

At this point you may wish to consider what format your message will be sent in: text-only, HTML or MIME/ Multi-Part format. HTML mail has the ability to strengthen your message by combining fully graphical images with text. Studies differ greatly whether HTML or text is more popular overall, but some trends have been established by non-partisan research. For instance, less experienced e-mail users tend to desire HTML mail, while more seasoned users seem to favor text-only. Still, it is advisable to allow subscribers to choose their desired format themselves. Recipient format preference can be stored in your database much like you would store other preference and demographic information.

A MIME or Multi-Part specification is intended to allow you to send messages in both text and HTML format. The recipient's e-mail programme then displays the format it can best view.

Your Message Out

As your e-mail marketing operations evolve and your mailings grow in size, it will become apparent that the task is too complex and requires too much manpower for your current system to handle. Select software that is capable of managing your lists as they grow and can measure the effectiveness of your campaign. Your software should have the ability to automatically remove bounced or undeliverable e-mail addresses from your list, as you may find the task of manually removing such addresses very time consuming and tedious.

— *Message Format Testing* - After crafting your message, it is important to test it to make sure it is properly formatted. Set up your own accounts using popular commercial providers, such as AOL, Yahoo! and Hotmail. Send yourself or your colleagues the test message to determine if formatting problems exist. If you are sending HTML mail, it is extremely important to check whether your message is viewable in both Microsoft Internet Explorer and Netscape browsers. If you are not technically savvy, it is advisable to consult your staff Webmaster or consult with a professional in this field.

— *Scheduling Delivery* - A valuable feature of advanced e-mail marketing and e-mail list management technology is the ability to schedule delivery for a specific time and date. This feature ensures that your message arrives in subscribers' inboxes at an opportune time. If you can determine whether you have a recipient's home or work e-mail address, scheduled delivery becomes even more valuable.

Evaluate and Revise Campaign

For best results, create a pilot campaign that tests the effectiveness of your message on a select portion of your database. Measure the results from the trial, make adjustments, and test another group. Refine your message until you feel comfortable enough to launch a full campaign.

Once you have sent your final message to recipients, you can begin to measure campaign results. Monitoring responses enables you to determine the quality of your recipient lists and the effectiveness of e-mail content. E-mail marketing programmes are capable of recording whether recipients open up your message, and if they do, whether or not they clicked on the embedded link included within the text. By being able to quantify these activities, you can measure the success of campaigns and, if necessary, make adjustments to achieve higher conversion rates. This is a key component of an e-mail marketing campaign.

Importance of Privacy

One of the biggest advantages of e-mail marketing is its ability to measure campaign effectiveness on the individual recipient level, unlike other advertising mediums such as print or television ads. However, your marketing objectives may not necessitate individual results gathering. Moreover, subscribers may not give their permission to perform such tasks, or your ability to do so may be curtailed by laws in certain jurisdictions. Therefore, it is important to understand what level of tracking procedures to impl-ement into your campaign.

Personal Tracking involves associating each individual event with the specific recipient who triggered it. If this method of measurement does not fit your marketing objectives, you may wish to choose Anonymous Tracking or Blind Tracking.

Once you have determined the method with which you wish to measure data, you need to choose your preferred method to view tracking data. You may wish to view results online in real time or download data into spreadsheet software, such as Microsoft Excel. With either option, you have the ability to create highly intuitive reports that help you evaluate the strengths and weaknesses of your e-mail marketing campaign.

Tips for Establishing a Successful E-Mail Marketing Campaign

Do:

— Build your list internally, even if it takes time, so the quality of your recipient list remains at a high level.

— Keep an accurate audit of how your company received permission to contact the subscribers of the lists - some people forget they signed up to receive information.

— Make membership to your list valuable by offering deals that nonmembers cannot receive.

— Make sure that your company's name is clearly stated in the domain name which appears in the "Sender" line of the e-mail.

— Use clearly stated words that describe what you want customers to respond to in both the "Subject" line and the body of your message.

— Provide recipients with a clear way to contact information, including a staffed telephone number or e-mail address.

— Provide subscribers with clear instructions of how to

be removed from future mailings, and make sure that your Privacy Policy is easily accessible.

— Plan mailings for specific, opportune times so subscribers are expecting your messages and are properly suited to respond.

— Personalise headers with recipients' names, and tailor messages that are ideally suited for different target segments.

— Choose software that is capable of performing as your lists grow, scans outgoing messages for viruses and can measure the effectiveness of your campaign.

Don't:

— Send messages to those who did not request to receive information.

— Purchase or rent lists from brokers who are not reputable.

— Use exclamation points, capitalised letters or other blatant marketing techniques that are synonymous with spammers.

— Send irrelevant offers to members of your database - for example, if you run an online travel agency, do not send special airfares incentives that originate from airports that do not correspond with the zip codes members have provided.

— Overload recipients with too many e-mails - only offer truly special deals.

— Cram too many messages into a single e-mail or send large attachments that may clog subscribers' inboxes.

— Neglect to test messages for formatting errors, especially when sending HTML messages or when contacting AOL users.

— Rely on your e-mail programme's spellchecker - have several colleagues proofread your message for spelling and grammatical errors.

— Sell or rent your e-mail lists to other organisation unless you have been given specific permission to do so.

— Expect every campaign will be an immediate home run - crafting quality messages takes time and requires feedback.

E-Mail Marketing Software Works

Many marketers prefer to concentrate less on the technical side of e-mail marketing and more on the content of the messages, it is important to have a basic understanding of how e-mail marketing software works. In order to efficiently conduct an advanced e-mail marketing campaign, it is essential to employ professional e-mail list management software. The software must be installed on a server with a dedicated connection to the Internet. Your Web site and database then communicate directly with the software. When someone visits your company Web site and signs up to receive your newsletter, the software will automatically add the e-mail address to an e-mail recipient list for future mailings.

Your e-mail list management software should have the ability to automatically handle all list subscriptions and sign-offs as well as bounced e-mail messages. The software should also be capable of connecting to your database and pulling out specific information about your recipients. This information can then be inserted into messages to create personalised mailings. More advanced software, capable of measuring campaign results, will provide your organisation with better opportunities to strengthen your marketing efforts. The ability to track e-mail responses is an important part of an e-mail marketing campaign because it allows you to determine how effective your campaign has been. By being able to rapidly quantify results, marketers can make instant adjustments to their campaigns and achieve optimal results.

Choose an E-Mail Marketing Solution

By 2006, more than $6.8 billion will be spent on e-mail marketing solutions. As the industry continues to grow, more and more vendors will offer products and services to satisfy the demand. But, as during the last few years, technology companies can disappear just as quickly as they enter the arena. How then can you be certain that your investment in e-mail marketing software and services will be sound? Here are a few key questions to consider before you decide to purchase an e-mail marketing solution:

Most likely, one goal of your e-mail marketing agenda will be to grow your list and perhaps create additional lists. If you purchase an e-mail list management solution and maintain a single mailing list with 1,000 subscribers, the product may not have the capability to function when your success dictates that you run five lists with 10,000 subscribers each. Set realistic expectations for where your e-mail marketing operation will be in one to two years from when you make the initial purchase, and determine whether the product will have the ability to handle the additional workload. Keep in mind that some software products can be purchased in increments and increased in capacity over time.

Imagine spending thousands of dollars on an e-mail marketing solution only to find that it will not work in conjunction with your database or other key applications. If you have previously invested heavily in customer database capabilities, finding an e-mail marketing software that seamlessly integrates with your database will save time and money.

Savvy IT professionals will evaluate a product on a trial basis before recommending it. Take advantage of the opportunity to evaluate e-mail marketing software before purchasing to ensure that it performs as advertised.

Installing any new technology product should be as painless a process as possible. Often, businesses cannot afford to tie up resources for extended periods of time during installation procedures. Have your organisation's technical staff the product's installation manuals to determine how much time and resources will be required to install the software or find out if the company offers installation/configuration services.

E-mail marketing software is sophisticated, and often marketers find that they are not taking full advantage of every feature. Extended training courses may be necessary to ensure that your organisation is getting the most out of its investment. Also inquire about the vendor's support policies, which should cover any technical difficulties you may encounter.

Marketers often want to outsource their e-mail marketing needs to companies that offer such services before bringing operations in house. Outsourcing is a sound temporary solution, especially for small companies that may not have the hardware, personnel or capital to license software initially. This arrangement also provides a trial period for marketers to determine if the software is worthy of licensing, which is typically a more cost-effective solution in the long run.

E-mail marketing software and services are among the most cost-effective solutions your company will invest in. However, vendors vary greatly in price and the features they offer. Have a clear idea of what features and functions you demand, and evaluate many different products. Also determine whether licensing or outsourcing makes business sense for your company.

Hosting vs. Licensing

Before selecting a solution, you must evaluate which arrangement will best suit your needs: hosting or licensing. If you choose to license software, you will conduct all operations on your premises. With hosting, e-mail marketing operations are run by another company that has expertise in that field.

CRM Solution to Conduct E-Mail Marketing Campaigns

The short answer is a resounding "no." CRM, or Customer Relationship Management, is a concept that has become well known over the last five years. The term 'CRM' is rather vague but can best be described as, "comprising of the methodologies, software, and Internet capabilities that help a company manage customer relationships in an efficient and organised manner." The downside of CRM solutions is not in principle, but in what they actually deliver for the price.

Without question, one of the most important elements of a customer relationship platform is e-mail marketing. However, this is where CRM solution providers fall short. According to the Aberdeen Group, companies that have invested in costly CRM solutions are disappointed with CRM's lack of functionality in this area. Aberdeen suggests that companies are now turning to true e-mail marketing technology suppliers to provide the mission-critical solutions that CRM vendors cannot offer.

Taking Action

Now that you have a solid foundation of knowledge for

what will be needed to achieve your e-mail marketing objectives, it is now time to begin capitalising on this innovative opportunity to drive sales, build company and brand awareness and build quality long-lasting relationships with customers.

Here is what you need to do:

— *Research Providers* - Web sites, white papers and industry analysts, such as Forrester Research, Aberdeen Group and Gartner Group, are the best places to start your search. Search engines should point you to the multitude of online product evaluators that have undoubtedly covered all the vendors you would be interested in. You may also want to check with trade organisations, such as the DMA, to make sure that the company you do business with is favourably recognised within the industry.

— *Investigate Possible Integration and Other Resource Problems* - If you have heavily invested in a customer database, eliminate any vendor from your list of candidates that cannot properly integrate its solution with your database. Also, make sure that you have the proper bandwidth, hardware and personnel in place to orchestrate a sizable e-mail marketing campaign. If not, perhaps an outsourced alternative is an appropriate solution.

— *Have a Plan to Acquire Subscribers* - Building an opt-in e-mail list is a challenge. Consumers are constantly bombarded with e-mail offers in their inboxes. Outline a plan to acquire subscribers that involves creating value and tailoring messages based on your customers' demographics, online history and preferences. Clearly define your privacy policy for recipients to gain their trust. Word of mouth is important in the online community, and news travels fast. Provide subscribers with quality offers, and they will pass along your messages to friends and colleagues.

— *Explore the Opportunities* - E-mail is a fantastic medium for marketing your products and services. E-mail is universally popular, reaches decision makers and is technologically advanced. Apply your marketing experience and expertise to the technology, and you will enjoy the results. It is that easy. If you are having trouble getting started, check out marketing trade magazines such as DM News and various American Marketing Association publications to read success stories and find ideas. The possibilities are nearly limitless, so trust your marketing skills and let the technology do its job.

L-SOFT PRODUCTS AND SERVICES

LISTSERV® E-Mail List Management Software

L-Soft's flagship product, LISTSERV®, was developed by L-Soft founder Eric Thomas in 1986 and was the first product created for managing e-mail lists. LISTSERV® enables users to administer any size e-mail lists - from as many as several million subscribers to as little as a few. LISTSERV® is currently used to manage more than 235,000 lists and delivers about 35 million messages per day. The software is available for Windows 2000/NT/XP; Unix: Solaris, Linux, AIX, Tru64, HP-UX, IRIX, FreeBSD, BSDi; OpenVMS and VM. Databases to which it can connect to include IBM DB2, Oracle®, MS SQL Server, MySQL and any ODBC-compliant database.

LISTSERV® Maestro

New to L-Soft's line of products, LISTSERV® Maestro complements LISTSERV® and provides organisations with advanced software technology for conducting e-mail marketing campaigns. LISTSERV® Maestro guides marketers through the steps of preparing e-mail campaigns for delivery: creating the message, assigning team responsibilities, selecting a targeted list of customers, testing and scheduling delivery and tracking responses.

LISTSERV® Maestro is available for Windows 2000/ NT and Unix.

— The easy-to-use Web interface guides marketers through each step of campaign development - from message creation to response evaluation.

— Marketers can choose the degree of personally identifiable information that is collected for tracking reports to protect the privacy of e-mail recipients.

— Marketers can view tracking data online in real time or download it for further analysis.

— LISTSERV® Maestro is compatible with other solutions and can be implemented rapidly.

— The outsourced LISTSERV® Maestro alternative is available for customers who want to manage and track e-mail marketing campaigns without hardware or software investments.

LSMTP® E-Mail Delivery Software

LSMTP® is the fastest e-mail delivery application available on the market. Clients with large e-mail workloads appreciate the performance and ease of use this software provides. A single server equipped with LSMTP® once delivered 1.87 million messages in an hour. The software is available for Windows 2000/NT and OpenVMS.

ListPlex® and EASESM E-mail List Hosting Services

ListPlex® and EASESM e-mail list hosting services provide customers with access to L-Soft's expertise and technology without hardware, software or personnel investments. Outsourcing services can be tailored to meet the needs of the largest newsletters on the Internet - or simply help hobbyists keep in touch with others sharing the same interests.

Training and Consulting Services

L-Soft offers comprehensive training and consulting services to improve customers' effective and appropriate use of electronic mail products and services. Customised training services help you achieve your objectives quickly and efficiently by streamlining the learning process and eliminating the frustrating trial and error that often accompanies deployment of enterprise software. Training classes are hands-on courses that are tailored to meet the needs of your individual organisation.

L-Soft also offers comprehensive consulting services, providing your organisation with in-depth customised assistance throughout the implementation cycle. L-Soft's consultants can help integrate products and services with your existing systems to more effectively address your e-mail needs and to produce measurable business results. Through needs assessment, planning, implementation, testing, optimisation and troubleshooting, L-Soft's co-nsultants will guide you toward meeting your e-mail objectives and achieving your business goals.

13

Future of Internet Marketing

The evolution of the virtual experience and the promise of cyberspace have recently begun to open doors to information which were previously inaccessible. Everyone from public universities to big business is racing to cash in on what promises to be the future of information and communications.

A totally paperless, highly-dynamic environment has been created in which ideas and images are exchanged free from the binds of the physical world. In this virtual space, there are no rules. There is no government regulation. What exists is the most massive amount of knowledge ever assembled on a common grid. It is for this reason that an internet connection is fast becoming the best way to reach the masses and provide input into a large percentage of the earth?s composite knowledge.

The implications of a digital tomorrow on the way man conducts his day to day affairs is astounding. How will the business traditions of the past fit into the binary stream of the future? The world of mass marketing is evolving at an alarming rate, and the vehicle which will bring the business of the future to the doorsteps of every American lies in the web of the internet.

Changing Face of Traditional Marketing

Mankind is currently standing on the verge of the greatest change in lifestyle which he has ever undertaken. All around the globe, businessmen and other enterpenuirs are racing to cash in on the future of marketing. Tradition is being turned on its head as all of free enterprise begins plans to phase out age-old methods of fiscal stimulation for the more powerful, more effective, and most cost-concious world of the internet. Their logic is not too difficult to understand.

Last year, American businesses spent billions of dollars advertising their products by magazine, newspaper, radio, television, and mass mailers. They flooded the homes of America, targeting every breathing carbon-based life form they could find, with countless jingles, images, song and dance in an attempt to peddle their often unwanted goods. This type of nuclear marketing (dropping a powerful load at a random percentage of the population) has been the backbone of corporate America.

Times, however, are changing. With the deregulation of the Internet in 1991, the federal government opened the doors of industry to the potential of advertising twenty-four hours a day, almost free of charge to anyone in the world who accessed their link. While it is true that this new advertising is not seemingly as direct, it does provide a marketing tool who directly targets interested parties. The largest problem with traditional marketing stems from the fact that, in order to determine who is interested in a product, the business would have to ask everyone.

Changes in information access are forcing the game to evolve. Now, businesses can enjoy presenting their product to those who seek them out. Moreover, this new media revolution costs almost nothing to set up. It is clear that traditional marketing is approaching a revolution. It is a twiching dinosaur who is awaiting his doom. As the world continues to interlink itself, business will alter the way in which it reaches its customer. Those who evolve will prosper. Those who do not shall perish.

The internet may seem like a whole new world to many citizens, but it is, in fact, based on the promise of a more efficient existence. Within the pages of the internet, the future of marketing, commerce, and retail lies. It will soon be the key to accessing millions of people, businesses, and services in a user-friendly, interactive environment. The inevitability of the internet lies in its great appeal to change the marketing strategies of corporate America. It provides marketing specialists with a gateway to not only the United States, but to the world. Imagine the vast amount of traditional resources necessary to introduce a product around the world. The cost of conventional advertising would make such an attempt futile.

In stark contrast, businesses choosing to market products and services with "cybermail" find that the internet reduces both the time and cost of traditional communications. The internet, then, offers greater accessibility, lower costs, and higher levels of efficiency than traditional marketing techniques. It better represents the interests of both the companies and those who they hope to serve. Internet advertising is more personal, more helpful, and more beneficial to society as a whole. With a simple click of a mouse, consumers can access informaiton of interest and not be subjected to useless random trajectory mailings.

The improved capabilities made possible by the internet web promise to revolutionize the world of tomorrow. With the net, there is no need to purchase a newspaper to read about daily events. A TV guide is not necessary to find the listings of popular shows. There will be no more hassles of getting the monthly bills out on time as all transactions can be performed in a digital medium. Credit Card companies, public utilities, banks, libraries, and retail establishments are all poised to position themselves in the new global marketplace. Shopping for cars, homes, and appliances is already possible on the net. It is easier and more profitable for all parties involved.

With the promise of a brighter fiscal tomorrow, corporate American stands ready to pounce on internet users and inundate them with product information on demand. The future holds a new digital marketplace in store for Americans. An existence in which everyday errands are underaken not in the family Caravan but through the modum and mouse.

Shopping, paying bills, entertainment, and banking are all ready to enter the American home through a more efficient channel, offering their services to the world for nominal cost in advertising. Interesting, many have noted, but how soon are we to see these changes appear on the net? The harbaringers of change are already in place and they promise to redefine the lifestyles of every man, woman, and child on the planet.

Information and Technology-Based Marketing

Information technology has two important effects for Marketing.

First, many firms now possess much more information about consumers' choices and reactions to marketing campaigns than ever before. However, few firms have the expertise to intelligently act on such information. The first goal of this course is to help students develop this expertise. Specifically, the course will teach what it takes to collect, analyze, and act on customer information. While we will use many quantitative methods in the course, the goal is not to produce experts in statistics. Instead, the goal is to train students to be able to comfortably interact with and manage a marketing analytics team.

The second effect of information technology is that it has changed the competitive environment for many firms: consumers have more information about competitive offerings, the Internet has allowed many competitors to market to consumers directly, and so on. Marketing is going through an evolution from having been primarily an art to becoming a science.

Transforming Entertainment Marketing

Digital Disney

A cataclysmic change in communicaitions and marketing promises to take place in the field of entertainment on the web. Recent innovations in digital media have enabled the entertainment industry to make their binary sequences available to all those interested, provideing them with yet another way to get their product to constomers. Case in point, the Buena Vista Movieplex and its on-line theatrical teasers. This site is set up as an alternative marketing method to publicize new movies for the Walt Disney company in an attempt to arouse the curiosity of the masses and reinforce feelings of product loyalty. What makes this site a useful marketing tool is the fact that it?s interactive multimedia environment provides a more personal experience for the user. Unlike traditional entertainment sections, on-line browsers may examine clips, soundbytes, and video stills from a number of possible films. This more personal marketing is a hallmark of the new digital marketplace.

Customers who actively search out a product will be much more willing to sift through trivial information. It is advertising which is entertaining for the user. When this fact is examined, it becomes immediately obvious that traditional marketing is no longer the most efficient way to present a product. In addition, the network makes financial sense to Disney. Information and advertising can be provided twenty-four hours a day for very little cost to the company, and has the promise to be much more effective than conventional advertising. It is for this reason that changes in marketing will revolutionize the free enterprise system in years to come.

Pathfinder

The evolution of the traditional magazine in self-marketing is interesting as it suggests the way in which conventional publicaitons will fight for self identity in the information age that is to come. Time Warner has developed its own on-line conglomerate of its magazines called Pathfinder. With it, the consumer can read electronic articles about the most current and up-to-date events without the hassle or cost of actually purchasing a magazine. In addition, they need only to spend time reading news in which are of particular interst. One might question the logic of Time Warner group in offering its publications free of charge, but it must be realized that by going on-line, the publishing giant increases its readership and becomes encamped as a player in the digital marketplace. The audience served by the internet is potentially larger than that served by traditional forms of circulation, and it offers an inexpensive vehicle to reach the masses.

In a world that's becoming ever more digital, Time Warner has initiated an intelligent marketing strategy by investing in the net. When newspapers, magazines, and radio become overshadowed by the power of the National Information Infrastructure, Time-Warner will already have created a successful home for itself on the net. Through Pathfinder, the mass public can easily and enjoyably learn more about current political and social news. This new digital medium is most certainly a look at the future of marketing, for both the politically and socially concerned.

Internet Movie Database

The internet movie database is yet another example that demonstrates the future face of marketing. Movie makers worldwide can advertise for thier films through this one, simple, and extensive site. In addition, the interaction made possible between consumer and producer in the database will enable movie-makers to create films that audiences are most interested in. Gone will be the days of tediously designing polls and questionnaires to guage audience desire and response; on the internet, people in the movie industry will talk and discuss cinema-related issues directly with the consumer. How will this benefit the consumer? By utilizing this site, an avid moviegoer has access to immense amounts of information on movies. Anyone with access to a computer and a modem potentially has access to this database. With it, bibliographies and filmographies on actors worldwide can be explored. Other exciting areas of this new marketing strategy include the movia trivia section and a series of interactive conferences discussing developing scripts. It is truly a database for the future of marketing.

No greater business exists than the US government, so even the Whitehouse is marketing itself on the internet. This is extremely logical as svoter percentages are down, and many citizens feel alienated by their government. The Whitehouse site enables users to interact with the officials who run the country. The internet provides a way for the government to become a more personal entity, and it also helps the government become more easily accessible.

This marketing stretegy makes it possible for the browser to gain information on new and debated issues of public policy. By making itself available of the internet, the government boosts its image and almost gains public support because now everyone in the world has access to the more personal side of the government. As we move towards an internet-based future, the government will coincide with the times. In the future, the presently overwhelming governmental system will become more accessible, understandable, and personable. This is all a reasult of marketing on the internet.

Special interest groups can also find marketing homes on the internet. Groups such as Earth First can make themselves more well known by using the net as an interactive component to thier publicity. Earth First is an environmental group concerned with many ecological issues. Whereas special-interest groups such as this may have difficulty informing large numbers of people about their activities simiply by mailing out flyers, self interest groups can market themselves on the net with little cost. Consumers may read of the group's activities, interests, and motivations. The internet provides groups such as Earth First with a larger market to appeal to, and it saves them time and money reaching the consumer. This greater exposure allows these groups to increase in size, and provides them an inexpensive way to learn about the nation and worldwide special interest groups.

The future of entertainment marketing will undoubltedly be littered with companies who attempt to lure new customers into their interactive advertising. Case in point, the interactive computer game used to publicize the new horror movie Demon Night. It was set up to allow the user to explore the set of the movie, meet major characters, and provide feedback to the directors on the potential outcome of the story while the film was still in production. This site illustrates the power the net may have in the future of entertainment. It is very possible that directors and studios will use such interactive games in order to test the market?s receptiveness to new story concepts.

In addition, a feeling of anxiousness can be formed around the release of a movie without any of the traditional high-cost meida vehicles (television, newspaper, and magazine advertising). This site serves as an interesting example of the future of marketing. It is concievable that a much better advertising campaign could be run through the net and an interactive game than could ever be run with conventional means. The evolution of the world of entertianment will undoubtedly be rooted in the Internet and a more personal style of advertising.

The internet network is becoming increasingly popular among businesses as an avenue for marketing their products and services. The system is growing rapidly, with twenty-five million users in ninteen-niney four, a number which is expected to increase over the years (LaMonica 57). An Internet expert predicts that the number of commercial users on the Internet will reach fifty million by ninteen nintety-eight (Cross 20); a fifty percent rise in only four years. What implications and effects are in store for the future of marketing with such a rapid advance in technology?

Experts express both concerns and breathless anticipation. This computerized information boom has enormous potential to boost economies world-wide, but it also has the possibility of being expolited. Advertising and marketing on the Internet makes obtaining huge profits possible. Id Software Inc., for example, sold several thousand copies of its Doom cliff-hanging software game the first weekend that it made the game available on the Internet.

The company now has sold about ten million dollars worth of software via the net, while avoiding the costs of overhead that generally consume profits. Sellers, though, are not the only ones to reap benefits from the internet. Purchasing products over the net is also beneficial. It is faster than the traditional process of mail ordering, and the on-line support forums provide advice that is not found in manuals, catalogs, or brochures. To have marketing success on the internet does not require the abandonment of traditional marketing methods; innovation and placement are the prime components in the formula for acquiring internet revenues.

Those businesses who devise a successful marketing plan are guaranteed a large profit for their efforts: commercial trade on the net is currently estimated at $200,000 per day, and is expected to substantially increase over the years. To make the network work to thier advantage, direct marketers have more to consider than just developing a sound financial plan of action. Internet experts lay out several suggestions to generate profit and be a net success.

Marketers should avoid being intrusive or sending unwanted messages, for practically noting else annoys internet users more. Instead, an affective approach is to use the internet for building higher levels of relationships with consumers through diaglog. Furthermore, Oglivy & Mather Direct has developed six rules for advertising on the Internet: consumers should only be given information which they have requested, data derived from a consumer interaction should never be resold, advertising should be limited to pre-specified newsgroups and list servers, promotion and direct selling must be preceded by full disclosure, consumers must be informed of end uses of market research, and communications software must not contain hidden functions. What does all of this mean for the future of marketing? The internet, as of now, is a free enterprise network.

Neither government nor big business owns or regulates its content or procedures, thus allowing for a liberal dissemination of information. The costs for marketers or purchasers to use the net is very low, thus enabling both groups to make or save money. There are, however, problems to consider in this cyberspace wonderland. Commercial interests are flocking to the internet, and are directing their aims to the distribution of services and information to mainstream commercial audiences. Marketers should, experts of the net worn, be more cautious before starting internet sites and pages. Rather than automatically assuming the benefits of the medium, they should realize that many Internet sites offer poor data. They are much less accessible than interactive TV services, and they often include outdated information.

Marketers should experiment with the medium but not blindly embrace it for the sake of their image. Rushing to set up shop on the web could be disasterous without the proper research and attitude, because the technology lacks such mission critical features as management, backup, security, and performance management. Some businesses, such as Pizza Hut, simply may not have internet-using customers; however, the low cost of setting up on the internet still remains a good argument in favor of doing so anyway.

A good guage of what advertisers should focus upon comes from what type of audience they are playing to on the internet. Net users want advertising to be informative. A reason for this advertising approach focuses upon an internet user profile with notes that internet users are predominantly educated, discerning individuals. A survey of internet users by a commercial marketing firm found that eighty-seven percent possess a college degree and sixty-seven percent earn more that 50,000 per year. What are the best ways for business to market goods and services on a computer network occupied by such individuals?

Experts on the use of the internet, some of whom have played major roles in linking its twenty-five million users, are uncertain. Some experts stress the unique cultural norms which are evolving among internet users as the best way for business to develop an internet customer base. Among the major barriers to successful marketing are security concerns and the absence of a definitive look and feel that will appeal to consumers.

While the net is viewed as more user friendly than interactive TV, transactions are, as yet, few because of technology hurdles. For one, the net is not a closed system, which raises concerns of security. In addition, the differing computers and networks that comprise the net makes develping transactions difficult. The internet also requires increased competitive effort from enterpeneurs because government bureauvcrats and their associated tax payer-supported groups will not provide the best information superhighway. This leads to widespread concerns that the internet will become a breeding ground for monopolies as groups struggle to gain the most control and profit from the net.

Future for Internet Marketers

Have you ever attended a class where the instructor followed the Socratic method of teaching? You remember, only questions, no direct answers. Some discussions lend themselves best to that format, and this look at some possible future trends in Internet marketing is one of them.

Mainly because there are no answers at this point, only the questions we pose!

Internet marketers by and large are used to creating products for, and selling to, a predominantly western audience. Whether inside the marketing niche or not, today's web sites, autoresponder sequences, mailing lists, payment processing systems, and overall way of doing business have evolved around the needs and wants of target markets in the western world. And any experienced marketer knows it can be difficult. Despite popular notions that you can start an Internet business and watch the money roll in, the reality is that there is a lot of competition from other webmasters, regardless of the market or type of products you promote.

Looking ahead, have you considered the impact of even more competition - lots more? In Asia, in particular China and India, large, well-educated populations, a lower cost of living with much-improved standards, and more widely available Internet access may combine in the near future to create a lot more Internet marketers. Many are well-versed in technical aspects of the Internet, including programming and site development. In fact, if you've ever used any of the various freelance sites to outsource technical projects, you've seen that many of the bidders are from Asia.

With populations of one billion people and more in those two countries alone, the current generation is certainly well-attuned to the Internet, and being avid surfers, are no doubt aware of the commercial opportunities and worldwide reach available only on the net. It's likely only a matter of time before they begin marketing to western audiences themselves.

Whether through affiliate marketing, or by developing new products to sell on their own behalf, the prospect of increased competition for current Internet marketers is very real, and likely very near. The biggest hurdles will be language and market understanding. After all, it's difficult enough to write effective sales letters in ones native language, even if addressed to a market and culture you understand. Over time, even those barriers will fall - face it, just as programming can be outsourced, so can marketing and language assistance.

The potential competition can sound ominous. And depending on your outlook, it can be. For every new product that pays affiliate commissions, there soon could be lots more marketers trying to promote it to the same audience. And for every new product of your own you develop, similar products with more features and selling for a lower price could appear. That already happens now to an extent. What will it be like with even more marketers and developers competing?

But change can also be good news. You as an individual marketer can either complain about the unfairness of it all, or you can choose to adapt your business to the inevitable and prosper. As new marketers, and surfers in general, from China, India, and elsewhere come online, they will also create entirely new markets to sell to, markets that weren't there just a short time ago. After all, as marketers they will need the same types of products and services that western marketers need. And as surfers and eventual online buyers, their consumers will want not only western, but also regional and cultural goods, just as online shoppers in the western world do now. Of course, marketers in those regions will also compete in their local markets, as well as western ones.

The globalization of Internet marketing will continue rapidly, no doubt about it. To stay in the game, western marketers would be well-advised to begin their strategic planning for this trend now. New markets and new opportunities are forming - learn to spot them at a distance through global binoculars!

Schemes, ideas and even secrets are available to the newcomer internet marketer, almost a new one every other day. It holds the promise of riches and a happy fulfilled life for just following a few simple steps. True it is, the steps are simple, but the profits lie beyond the steps as many disgruntled internet marketers have by now realized. The internet business is not an easy money generating machine for just anyone who dares enter.

What many people trying to make it in the *internet marketing business* tend to forget, mainly because of very well written and researched sales letters, is that the online business is relatively the same as an off-line business. You can't run an off-line business working two hours a day and make a ton of cash. Any business needs time to grow with ups and downs, it has always been like that and it will always remain like that.

The autopilot has retired quite some time ago and if you figure that you want to employ him get ready to pay his retirement fund. Ok this so far sounds like someone who has now become fed up with the online marketing idea and the making money quick schemes. So why would you still want to pain yourself if there is no future? Guess what, there is a very lucrative future in the internet business you must just learn to see it. Opportunities are as abundant in the internet marketing arena as they have never been before and it is growing daily. More and more people are finding themselves able to work from home and earn a substantial income online.

So is there a secret to this that someone should write a book about? No, you already know the answer. It is plain simple hard work, divided into building your website with quality content, getting back links from authority sites and writing articles and posting them to the article directories.

Next step is to monetize your website, not castrate it. Decide on a product you would like to promote and add it to your site. Place the ad in a good position and do a small write up on the product. A interested visitor can click on the link and off they go to the sales page If they like the product and have the means to pay you have made a sale. It is as simple as that. There are many ways and means to get products and amongst them are resell rights products, PLR products, Affiliate products or your own product.

But remember, your sales will only come from traffic, feet as it is referred to in the off-line world. No feet, no traffic, no sales. So the secret here is no secret at all, get visitors to your site and you will make money. Make sure your on-page and off-page optimizations are done to the maximum of your ability and then add another one hundred percent of effort to make it better. The most effective way in which to get your pages indexed in the search engines and ranked is with article submissions to the article directories. From them you will receive one way back links, the most important links of all. They are the ones that will give you page rank and good search result placement.

The best place to be is at the top of page one for your search term, it is never easy but neither is it impossible. Have a look, there is someone in position one, and always will be. Why can it not be you?

FUTURE TRENDS AND FORECASTING

The way that business is being conducted worldwide is changing dramatically with the growth of the Internet.

Internet has made the world smaller in terms of reach and communication. Geographical distances do not matter anymore. Businesses are instantly reaching out to customers, distributors, suppliers, and employees sitting on the other side of the globe, thanks to the Internet. Internet marketing is the mantra for business success today because of the global access it provides. Sharing of information and ideas has never been this economical since businesses can have access to any website worldwide.

Large numbers of people are making use of the Internet and online businesses for making money and earning a living. We all know that the Internet is a fast-changing environment and we have new technological advancements every day. If you want to pursue internet marketing as a long-term business, it is important that you should know the future of Internet marketing, understand the emerging trends and be able to do future forecasting. This way, you can stay ahead of the competition and emerge a winner in Internet marketing.

You can even add testimonials to your audio file. It lends credibility to your website. Ask some of your satisfied customers to record their testimonials in audio format. It is an effective way to promote your website and the business that it represents. You can put the audio on your sales page for visitors to listen to what users of your product or services have to say. A link to your website in your email will also direct traffic to your website.

Another step forward is to have audio emails. You can send audio files along with your emails on the same lines that e-greeting cards do. A well-recorded and well-prepared audio file will work wonders for your sales campaign. Along the same lines, you can have audio newsletters sent to your existing and potential customers. Listening to a recorded message is more convenient for the customer than reading. A recording with the right emotional pitch thrown in can sway a prospective customer your way.

Podcasting

Podcasts are all set to rule the future trends of Internet marketing. Podcasts are available for almost all subjects under the sun and Podcasting is no longer an exclusive domain of the music and entertainment industry professionals. People are now looking for and downloading Podcasts on a wide range of subjects. Internet marketers can take the cue for this growing popularity of Podcasts and include Podcasting in their present as well as future Internet marketing strategy.

Role of Video

Similarly, video can be used to great effect. Video has an even better influence on your existing and would-be clients than audio does. Visual presentation has a lasting impact on the mind than audio. You can have video files placed on your website demonstrating the benefits of your products or services. You can also demonstrate how to use your products or services. Video testimonials have an even more telling effect on visitors on your site. Video presentations can help the visitors make up their mind about your product or services quickly.

As in the case of audio, you can have links posted in your emails or newsletters that directly take the recipients to your website containing video presentations. With broadband widths available freely, playing video is getting more convenient over the Internet.

Video blogging

The use of Video blogging as tool of Internet marketing cannot be ruled out. Just as we have audio blogs or

Podcasts, there is an immense scope for video blogs on the Internet. Video blogs are going to rule the Internet marketing domain because of the picture and sound advantage. A video blog is the perfect way of communicating message effectively and/or attracting potential customers. Video blogs and even video based contextual advertising on the Internet is set to gain popularity. With the broadband Internet becoming a norm, the popularity of video and audio blogs is set to increase by leaps and bounds.

Video blogging and advertising has a definite edge over plain text and audio Podcasts. However, the introduction of video and audio as a replacement of or a better alternative to textual WebPages is still a distant dream because of quality and speed related issues. Moreover, there are many other technological issues that need to be resolved before audio and video make a permanent place for themselves in the realm of Internet marketing.

Internet marketing is poised for a big growth with emerging technologies being incorporated in a big way. There was a time when audio and video on the Internet were not even distant possibilities. But, with the introduction of newer technologies, it appears that Internet marketing techniques are on the verge of radical change for the better. So, it will be to your advantage to gear up in advance for the emerging trends and be there when the Internet marketing boom occurs.

According to trend watchers of Internet Marketing, the near future will see websites getting more personalized as they cater to niche markets and consumers. Internet marketing through audio newsletters will become a more convenient tool for the target audience. An audio file can be placed with an html code easily. Herein the experts also foresee enhanced usage of podcasts, personalized and interactive audio newsletters and WebPages.

Role of Audio

If you are selling products and services on your website, you can simply add audio onto your sales letter. People tend to retain sounds more readily in their memory than the material they read. Reading material is cold and impersonal, whereas well-spoken words are warmer and more personal. It is easier to influence your prospective customers through your audio.

Bibliography

Ebbs, Geoffrey and Howard Rheingold. "Censorship on the Information Highway." *Internet Research: Electronic Networking Applications and Policy* 7, 1, 1997.

Elmer-Dewitt, Philip. "Fire Storm on the Computer Nets." *Time Magazine* 146, 4, July 24, 1995.

Feldman, Susan. "Power Tools on the Internet: Ghosts of the Net Yet to Come." *Searcher: The Magazine for Database Professionals* 4, 9, October 1996.

Floridi, Luciano, "Brave.Net.World: The Internet as a Disinformation Superhighway?" *The Electronic Library* 14, 5, October 1996.

Gellene, Denise, "Internet Marketing to Kids Is Seen as a Web of Deceit." *Los Angeles Times,* March 29, 1996: A1, A20.

Glasner, Joanna, "Internet Filtering Faces the First Amendment." *Law Journal EXTRA!,* September 29, 1997.

Strangelove, Michael and Diane Kovacs, Accessing God: Finding the Lord on the Internet." *Online Access,* November 1993.

____________ "Ad Age Finally on the Web." *The Internet Business Journal.* Volume 3, Number 3. March 1996.

____________ "Advertising on the Internet: Frequently Asked Questions and Answers." *Edge: The Entrepreneur's Magazine.* Fourth Quarter 1994.

____________ "Advertising on the Internet: Myths, Facts and Tips." *The Internet Business Journal.* Volume 1, Number 6. December 1993.

_____________ "Advertising on the Internet: Why Most Will Fail." *The Internet Business Journal.* Volume 1, Number 5. November 1993.

_____________, "At Play in the Fields of the Internet." *Online Access.* September 1993.

_____________ "The Commercialization of the Internet: Catching the Ear of Ten Million Users." *Online Access.* July 1993..

_____________ "Confessions of an Art Thief." *Online Access,* July 1995.

_____________ "An Electronic End to Censorship." *Online Access.* November 1994.

_____________ "Using the Internet for Marketing: A Publisher's Secrets." *Journal of Scholarly Publishing.* Volume 25, Number 4, July 1994.

_____________ Venditto, Gus, "E-mail Face Off." *Internet World* 7, 12, December 1996.

Wallace, Jonathan D., "Purchase of Internet Blocking Software by Public Libraries Is Unconstitutional: A Briefing Paper." *Australasian Public Libraries and Information Services* 10, 4, December 1997.

Index